The Journey Within

The Journey Within
Prayer as a Path to God

Sr. Kathryn James Hermes, F.S.P.

PUBLISHED BY ST. ANTHONY MESSENGER PRESS
CINCINNATI, OHIO

Cover design by Candle Light Studio
Book design by Phillips Robinette, O.F.M.

ISBN 0-86716-611-8

Servant Books is an imprint of St. Anthony Messenger Press.

Published by St. Anthony Messenger Press
www.AmericanCatholic.org

04 05 06 10 9 8 7 6 5 4 3 2 1

Printed in the United States of America

Contents

Introduction

There is a history behind this book, a history I share with the rest of humanity. It is the story of the experience of the void and the Holy, of disillusionment and meaning, of loneliness and love. We flee from one to the other, avoiding the feelings and situations that remind us of disappointments, buried dreams and broken relationships. If there is one thing listening to the hearts and prayers of others has taught me, it is that we most fear to be alone and unwanted.

In RCIA programs, prayer groups, seminaries and novitiates, people are taught the methods and ways of prayer. Eager pray-ers begin to follow the directions they have received and avidly read in books on spirituality. Even businesses have cashed in on spirituality as an attempt to deal with the over-taxed nervous systems symptomatic of a hurried society on overload. Often, in the end, however, this grasp at the mystery of the divine collapses. Why?

The answer to this question is the purpose of this book. In three movements, these chapters guide the reader first into the mystery of life in order there to discover the mystery of God. Is there a purpose for the upheavals we experience in life? How do we deal with the meaninglessness and nothingness we encounter? How is it that the human spirit moves from loneliness to love?

James Loder, professor of the philosophy of Christian education and author of *The Logic of the Spirit: Human Development in Theological Perspective,* believed that the upheavals that disrupt our lives are signs that "the human spirit inside us is seeking the Face of God to make up for the mother's face we have missed since infancy."[1] In mid-life we begin to reappraise our lives lived within and molded by a production-oriented society. Issues of generativity and care become important to us. We look back over the years and find that there are more disappointments and painful events than we realized. Often because these memories are painful or signify to us our failure we push them out of view. We split them off from who we are, pretending they aren't there. The energy of these hidden memories shows up in anxiety and all kinds of attempts to prove to ourselves that we are on top of things. And prayer, though we may continue to say prayers, can be strangled by the urgent power of these "forgotten" events of our history. We wonder why our relationship with God isn't as warm and real as we desire or as it once had been. We look around in vain for the transformation that God's presence promises.

It was one morning when I was feeling out of sorts and writing down the thoughts and feelings that were making me feel uncomfortably vulnerable that I unexpectedly bumped into such memories of my own. Illness, misunderstanding, fractured relationships...I connected the dots through the years. And as the dots increased and the lines grew longer, I grew more angry. I thought, *Why had God let these things happen? Why had God done this to me?* I didn't want anything more to do with a God who had messed things up so much. How could I trust the rest of my life to such reckless care?

From that moment on I began the painful process of bringing these memories and emotions with me before God. Until then I had pushed them away, and appeared before God in prayer with the best of myself. I couldn't totally give myself over to God, however, until I appeared before God with *all* of myself. It was the beginning of a new journey of wholeness and the prerequisite for authentic holiness—the discovery of God's tenderness for me and others. I marvel as I see this dynamic repeated again and again in others who share with me a part of their story.

We can encounter in hope the void and "quiet desperation" that are often the foundation of many of the achievements of our life. We can then proceed to the discovery of the one thing necessary: *that we are loved.* We encounter our loneliness to discover how to love.

Three Movements

There are three movements that lead us from loneliness to love. The first is naming the journey. Until we are introduced to the breadth and length of the Christian life, we can find our spiritual growth stunted. The theology of baptism, the primacy of a Love that has poured himself out for us, the promise of the end of the ages form the bedrock of our Christian life and of our prayer. People find prayer ineffective or tiresome when they seek to make the journey of the spiritual life without having received this foundation. The first movement, therefore, seeks to answer the question of why prayer withers over time by providing this strong foundation from the church's treasure house. It is as if the church were a pharmacy stocked with all types of medication and means of healing, but somehow the word hasn't gotten out. Few know where or how to find this treasure. The first movement opens the doors of the church's treasures and hands out the healing salves and ointments of which she is the minister.

The second movement looks closely at the lives of individuals seeking the mystery of God and discovering it in the midst of the mystery of everyday life. With these stories are woven passages of Scripture—the stories of salvation history that can shed light on and generate new life in our own stories of salvation.

The third movement returns to where many started out on a life of prayer: the discipline of abiding in the Word and contemplation. A spiritual director who walked with me through a significant part of my own journey did me the favor of planting me in the fertile soil of God's Word. He would pick up on one thread of what I had said and then read and explain some verses of Scripture that offered light and guidance. The first few times I was disconcerted when he would ask, "Is there something in Scripture that could help you?" Soon I realized that, whether I could think of anything or not, there certainly was *always* something he could point out in the Scriptures that could speak to my experience no matter where I found myself. Therefore, the third movement includes not only a primer on prayer methods, but guidance for opening up the Word of God in order to find something there "that could help you." A homesickness for Scripture would be the greatest gift you could acquire from reading this book.

Breaking Open Your Life

Because prayer is a relationship, this is not a "how to" manual. Authentic relationships are muddy and messy, and prayer is no exception. It is only the person willing to risk plunging into the mess who discovers that he or she is loved and lovable.

The astute reader will notice that these chapters are nonlinear. There is no map, no recipe, no directions when it comes to prayer. The Spirit is not confined to our poor, proud logic. The Spirit works outside of our control. Like a deep-sea diver who delves into the darkness of the ocean depths, the Spirit delves into the unknown parts of our inmost being, discovering pearls of great price we never knew were there.

The sections throughout the chapters entitled "Breaking Open Your Life" are exercises for journaling or prayer that are meant to help you open your inmost being to the illumination and healing of the Spirit. You will want to have a journal near you when you read so that you can respond to the exercises as part of your journey of prayer. It could also help to share what you have discovered with a spiritual director. It is a rule of the spiritual life that it is foolish to travel alone. Delusions and traps can too easily derail our sincerest attempts to pray. I encourage you to find a long-term consistent companion on your journey in a friend, soul mate, spiritual director or member of a prayer group. You may want to share some of the Breaking Open exercises with him or her.

There is no logic or organization to the Spirit's work, for God's ways are far above our own. The chapters of this book are adventures of the Spirit, probing your soul, bringing various facets and gifts of your personality and soul to light, opening them up to transformation, almost without your knowledge. As you read the chapters, let go. Curb the jealous control with which you guard your life. Enter the unknown. Let go of the logic that seeks a map, a beginning and an end. Let the Spirit work.

We Are Wanted

Andrei Rublyov's masterful icon *The Holy Trinity* became one of my favorite icons since a retreat I made some time ago. The icon was displayed in a tiny prayer room next to the tabernacle, and I spent many hours there in prayer.

In the icon there are three angels, representing the three persons of the Trinity. They are seated around a table. I think I was drawn to the icon by its striking stillness, as if the three persons were frozen in time. At the same time, there is in the picture a sense of warmth and life that circulates among the persons of this Trinity, extending out to include the person at prayer. The stillness in the picture quickly brought me to quiet. I didn't know what the iconographer had intended to express by the position of the angels, what they were communicating by their posture towards one another, and their arrangement around the table in relation to the person gazing at the icon. But I did know that I saw them as frozen yet alive, still yet warm, silent yet resounding an invitation. They lived in an eternal Now. They were offering an invitation to me. The three are seated to the left and right of the table, and the one in the back faces the person at prayer. There is a place for one more at the table. There is a place for me, I thought. I am welcome here. I am wanted. I have been thought of. I am being drawn into this mysterious relationship. I am being called forth into love.

Note:

[1]James Loder, class notes taken by Herbert Armstrong: Faith and Human Development (Pasadena: Fuller Theological Seminary), July 31, 2001.

Movement One
Naming the Journey

We come to prayer wanting God to love us, yet holding back in case he doesn't. We don't want to trust too much, because the pain of rejection would be too great. It would affirm what we already fear about ourselves: that we aren't lovable and, in fact, even God can't love us. We are alone and on our own. Do we fear anything more than this cosmic loneliness?

CHAPTER ONE

Clearing Away the Mental Clutter[1]

There are the voices which we hear in solitude, but they grow faint and inaudible as we enter into the world.

—Ralph Waldo Emerson, *Essays: First Series*

Solitude is the treasured place for encountering the divine. Jesus sought the solitude of the midnight sky or the mountains as his preferred place of prayer. Hermits and monks and nuns journeyed into the desert. In the silence and the lonely terrain they communed with God and fought the demons within their hearts. People of wisdom throughout the ages found time to muse, to ponder, to spend time alone. Scientists, artists, poets, and musicians know the many hours of silence that precede a breakthrough to creative ideas.

How do we find such moments for ourselves—these moments for prayer, for reflection, for creative leisure—when we are saturated with images, e-mails, sounds, information, virtual relationships, and instant messages? The blur between one activity and another has not created more time for leisurely contemplation, as once promised by these marvelous computers that could do more in less time than we humans. The

Internet, beepers, cell phones, and PalmPilots have expanded our careers so that they demand more attention, not less, for more time during the day, every day of the year.

There is no vacation from information. We are on information overload, stressed out by the inability of the human brain and nervous system to process everything. Even with regular time set aside for prayer, you may find it impossible to focus, to calm down, to become aware of God's presence for even a few moments.

Breaking Open Your Life

Make a list of all the electronic communications equipment in your life, including phones, beepers, voice machines, cell phones, PalmPilots, radios, TVs, teleconferencing equipment, Internet, e-mail and so on. What percentage of your time is tied to one form or another of electronic communication? How many e-mails do you answer a day? How often do you read or view the news? How much time a day or week are you *not* connected to one of these means of communication? How are they interfering with a deeper, more fulfilling sense of human or spiritual interaction?

Steps to Silence

How can we clear away the mental debris that clutters our hearts, the images, the emotions stirred by various situations, the ever-lengthening to-do list? Clearing away the mental debris is one of our most effective prayer supports.

Clearing away the debris—"draining your brain"—will help renew your ability to experience the personal presence of God.

If you are serious about prayer, consider doing a brain drain exercise. It's simple. Write two or three pages in the form of free association, stream of consciousness, mental clutter, and random memories or thoughts. Write quickly, don't look back, don't fix your spelling or your grammar, don't reread what you write. Just keep scribbling across the page.

Write any thought that comes to you. If you don't like writing out your thoughts, write that. If someone bugged you at the office, write about that. If you wish you were different, write about that. If you forgot to pick up milk at the store, write about that. Stop mid-sentence and start a new thought if something suddenly pops into your head. Write until you have nothing left to write about, and then write about having nothing left to say. Write for as long as it takes to clear away the storms, debris, emotions and memories.

When you finish, you will discover that your mind and heart are silent. There are no words, no memories, no forgotten things that you need to write down before the thought escapes you. You have returned to silence with hardly any effort. This exercise is most effective when done daily or at least several times a week. As you continually sweep away the turbulence, you discover that you are greater than the turbulence. You feel within yourself a depth and beauty. There is an inner longing that you couldn't experience when you were caught in random thoughts and memories and emotions.

I spent too many years assuming that what I thought and felt, emotions that held my mind and heart captive, were moral issues that defined me as good or bad. These unruly thoughts and emotions held me hostage. I made choices under the influence of these bandit sentiments that hid from me my true identity. This false self triumphed over my true self and I grew more frightened and weak.

Breaking Open Your Life

Every day for a week, spend fifteen to twenty minutes writing a stream-of-consciousness diary such as the one described above. Include every thought, concern, and emotion. Get it all out on paper. Just observe what is there, without reacting to it emotionally. Do you note any difference in your ability to focus?

Inner Voices

These unruly thoughts and emotions remain an undifferentiated mist as long as they are unconscious. When you name them, however, they become conscious and lose their power. This is not an exercise in psychology, it is simply setting one's house in order.

Perhaps an example would clarify what I mean. When I go home for vacation, my eight nephews and nieces usually come over to my parents' house. When my brother's four girls and my sister's four boys were between the ages of one and ten and everyone piled into my parents' house, bedlam broke out. The children seemed to be in control of the house until my Dad reasserted his authority. He called the children by name. He set limits. He encouraged good behavior. He identified what was unacceptable in his house. The children would settle down because they knew who the head of the house was and what he expected.

It's the same when we reassert order in the house of our inner being. If thoughts of jealousy, feelings of inferiority, demands for attention and respect rule the roost, you can expect your house to be chaotic. It does no good to try to pretend these inner voices aren't there or to squelch them. Both of these ways of dealing with the inhabitants of our heart only strengthen their power, even if they delay their next appearance.

Instead, we need to acknowledge them and call them by name. For example, within me there might be a Terrified Tina who is inordinately frightened when she gets into uncontrolled situations. There also might be a Don't-Step-on-Me-Dora who roars like a lion when someone gets in her way. Or Controlling Connie who needs to keep everything inside a box in order to feel safe, and Overwhelmed Alice who begins to panic when work piles up. Along with these voices, however, you will also hear the voices of grace: Patient Pam, Let's-Give-It-Time Tom, Gracious Greg, Hope-filled Hannah, Trusting Tanya. Your brain drain should eventually include a space for these voices to be heard. As you remember incidents that you haven't quite processed, you will start to hear all these voices. You can write out their names and what they are saying, using as much imagery and as many metaphors and descriptive phrases as possible.

You might feel overwhelmed as you write out what these inner voices say and relive the strength of out-of-control voices within. Let them all speak their contradictory, sometimes senseless, words. Writing these words down drains them of power. It allows you to notice the voices of grace and goodness, which are too often overwhelmed by the negative voices. In a short time you will realize that you are not your anger, your jealous thoughts, your frustrated feelings. You will sense that you are filled with grace, graciousness, and the Lord's love. You are more than all of these voices put together or any one of them taken alone.

As you put order in your house and sense the depth and beauty of your soul, you will find that the hard edges of these strident inner voices, so often driven by fear, become gently rounded and soft. Angry demands for self-protection disappear as trust for life grows. As negative inner voices lose their power and their fascination and positive voices grow stronger, you are free to begin a search for your true self. Your false self is gently unmasked as you realize that you are so much more.

You can establish order among the chaotic voices within, decide which, if any, voices you wish to follow, set limits on negative voices, and reward the good voices.

When the house is silent, you can go in to meet God.

Breaking Open Your Life

Take about ten minutes a day over several days to begin to name the inner voices that occupy your house. It will probably be easier to name the negative voices. If you need help hearing the voices of grace within you, call to mind the times when people expressed their appreciation for who you are or what you've done. They are expressions of the grace within you, places where God is at work in your life.

Note:

[1]Material in this chapter is adapted from a practice which is a tool of creative emergence originated by Mark Bryan with Julia Cameron and Catherine Allen in their book, *The Artist's Way at Work: Riding the Dragon: Twelve Weeks to Creative Freedom* (New York: William Morrow, 1998).

CHAPTER TWO

Moving from Violence to Reverence

In self-dispossession the heart is at rest.
It wants nothing.
Because it is grounded in Jesus
not on itself.

—St. John of the Cross, quoted in *Ascent to Love: The Spiritual Teachings of St. John of the Cross*

W hy is it that we think we need to be better than we are? The sign, "Be patient, God isn't finished with me yet," really means, "You won't like me today, but wait until tomorrow. I'll be better. I'll be improved." Improved. Revised. New edition. Even spirituality has fallen for the technological utopia: we will be saved by spiritual progress! What would happen if we said, "Rejoice in what you see, in what I am right now, an imperfect, immensely loved creature. God doesn't find it beneath his dignity to live in me."

But what about people who are sinning, or hurting others, or spreading scandal? How can God love them just as they are? Many people can't get over the notion that God loves best those who are good, or those who are trying to get better. Therefore, God loves me (if I think I'm pretty good), or God loves others and not me (if I can't believe I'm any good at all). There is no way out of this quagmire except through some psychological healing to better our self-esteem. We often find no way out, because many of us are missing most of the information we need to understand our Christian life.

If we focus on God instead of ourselves, we will find the answer to the problem. God is always in the same posture with regard to us. He is always facing us, always giving us the free offer of saving justice. "For God so loved the world that he gave his only Son, so that everyone who believes in him may not perish but may have eternal life" (Jn 3:16). God is always turned toward us, always giving.

I remember a teacher who illustrated this very simply. He picked up a book and offered it to a student. Before she reached up for it, he said, "Stop." Then turning to the class he said, "Is this book I'm giving to her a gift?" We all said it was. "No, it isn't," he replied. Then he asked the student to take the gift, "Is it a gift now?" he asked the class. Again we said yes. "No, it isn't," he said. It is only a gift when the receiver of the gift acknowledges that it is gratuitous, not deserved.

Gift by its very nature is a relationship. There is a free giver, a free recipient, and in the very act of reception an acknowledgement of the gratuity of the gift. The free gift of God gives me eternal life.

God's posture toward us is always a giving posture; it never changes. We may accept or refuse what he offers, but that doesn't change God's desire to bestow on us his Son. What does it mean to receive the gift of the Son? Does it mean to sing carols around the manger on Christmas? Or to spend Advent in a spiritual and noncommercial spirit? Does it mean to be super-religious? No. To accept the gift of the Son means simply to love him.

And how do we love him? The Gospel of John again makes the very simple claim that to love Jesus, we must obey his commands (cf. Jn 14:21-23).

What happens when we obey the commands of Jesus? Jesus said that he and the Father would make their home in that person's heart (cf. Jn 14:23).

And what happens when God makes a person's heart his home? Ahh. Here we need to stop our barrage of questions. From the inside-out Jesus makes it possible for us to love him, to obey his law, to taste his delights, to desire more of his life. In other words, Jesus himself obeys in us, desires in us, prays in us, lives in us, thinks in us, speaks in us.

An Attitude of Reverence

Instead of resolutions, this mystery calls for reverence. For the more we enter into prayer, the more Jesus is free to live in us. It is true that this is a gradual process. Even St. Paul spoke of himself as being within this process: "When I was a child, I spoke like a child, I thought like a child, I reasoned like a child; when I became an adult, I put an end to childish ways. For now we see in a mirror, dimly, but then we will see face to face. Now I know only in part; then I will know fully, even as I have been fully known" (1 Cor 13:11-12). But right now, wherever I am in this process, *I am inhabited by God!* God loves me! Wherever I am is okay. I can be gentle with myself because my eternal salvation doesn't depend on completing the process. It depends on accepting the gift. And if today I have accepted this gift, today I taste what it is to be a member of the household of saints (cf. 1 Cor 1:2).

Breaking Open Your Life

Here is an exercise you can do right now to begin this process.

Write down ten positive things about yourself. If you can't think of enough, do this exercise with a friend. Keep writing until you have ten. The faster you write the more characteristics will come to mind. Then write ten gifts God is giving you today.

Making Peace with What Is

One difficulty in prayer is coming to this reverence. We do violence to ourselves when, in an angry spirit, we grow frustrated with our weak and sinful hearts. What would happen if we could *reverently* approach job loss, an *F* on our child's report card, illness, even war. We can be gentle even in the face of evil.

We don't realize how little we actually pray until we become aware of how much of our prayer time is actually spent solving our problems, nursing our ideas of how others should change or improve, and coming up with ideas for transforming situations. It is true that all these can be inspirations, and I truly believe we need to pay attention to great ideas, especially when they come during times of prayer. Sometimes, however, this intellectual activity can actually sap our prayer life, because we end up trapped in the creative imagination or nursing our pouting heart.

Gentleness is the fruit of making peace with life as it is. The bold dreams and plans of youth give way to the ability to accept life in all its present reality. This is a typical movement of midlife. It can signal a transformation that is happening through prayer.

Breaking Open Your Life

Find a poem or a piece of art that represents gentleness to you and keep it nearby. Think about it. Contemplate it. Let it speak to your spirit.

For example, I like the opening lines of the poem *Desiderata* by Max Ehrmann: "Go placidly amid the noise and haste, and remember what peace there may be in silence."[1]

Effects of Prayer

There is a certain trajectory in prayer. When you consistently put aside time for it, three things happen. First, you become accustomed to the idea of prayer and notice the effects it has on your life. Second, your prayer results in the first steps toward taking on the mind and heart of Christ and frees you from the stress that hitherto dominated your life. Third, you begin to develop a noticeable radiance that overflows to those around you.

It is only as your prayer deepens, however, that you discover how much you have marshaled the power of prayer around your own ideas and needs. You refuse to accept situations or persons for what they are, for example, and so prayer becomes the means to solving life's problems and resizing others to fit your viewpoint.

This is a chronic problem in Christian life. From complaints about Sunday's homily to gossip about a mother-in-law's attitude toward her daughter-in-law, we find numberless ways to occupy ourselves without having to do the hard work of connecting to God and responding to his call.

At a certain point, however, the seriousness of your desire calls forth a greater outpouring of God's power in your soul. The Holy Spirit, in myriad ways, begins to give you a nudge here or a shake there: "You really think a lot of yourself." "Why do you think she has to be just like you?" "So you think everybody else is mediocre compared to you?" The Spirit nudges for weeks, months, years, very gently. The Spirit's desire is not to humiliate you. It is to open you.

Judgments, suspicions, cynicisms, impositions of your viewpoint leave you dissatisfied on the deepest level of your being, even if they yield short-term results. They arise from hardened viewpoints that are unable to imagine different possibilities. The Greek philosopher Epictetus said, "People are disturbed not by things but by the view they take of them." Those with hardened mindsets see life as serving their personal agendas.

But prayer, over the years, can pry open the closed mind to the dance of the Spirit. This happens as we realize, at a certain point, that God isn't validating *our* views and ideals. Instead he is asking us to give them up along with the hardness of spirit they create.

The easiest way to be moved by the Spirit through this transformative night is to pray *for* gentleness *with* gentleness, for trust in what is. Pray and keep on praying. This trusting prayer moves us beyond criticism or demanding change in others.

The writer James Ogilvy said, "I have come to believe that a life enslaved to one Goal, no matter how noble, becomes a mechanism rather than an organism, a business plan rather than a biography, a tool rather than a gift."[2] Instead we can live our lives with what the beloved convert Cardinal John Newman once called "a poetical view."

―――

Breaking Open Your Life

Take some time for personal prayer.

In a place of silence, remember the presence of God within you and all around you.

Breathing in, pray: I breathe in God's gentleness.

Breathing out, pray: Breathing out, I smile.

Repeat for your entire period of prayer.

―――

Note:

[1] Max Ehrmann, *Desiderata: A Poem for a Way of Life* (New York: Crown Publishers, 1995).
[2] James Ogilvy, *Computists' Weekly*. Vol. 10, No. 07, February 29, 2000, pp. 64-65

CHAPTER THREE

Relishing Life's Insecurity

Humility is the ability to recognize the glory in the clay of me.
—Joan Chittister, O.S.B., *Seeing with Our Souls*

Recently, two of my projects were handed over to others and no one told me why. On one level I knew that in both cases the other individual had more to give to that specific project than I. On another level I desperately tried to convince myself that the work I had done in initiating the project was still worthwhile. Attending meetings with these new project leaders, I found myself wanting to defend decisions I had made and justify what I had done. The changes benefited the projects and ultimately freed me for what I do best, but seeing my work handed over to another began to dismantle my illusion of domination and invulnerability.

We build illusions to hide from ourselves the fact that we are defenseless against so many things. We have the illusion of safety, of security, of financial stability. It takes one tragic incident to shatter it all. What do we get out of holding on to these illusions?

In these years following the terrorist attacks in New York City and Washington, D.C., I carry in my heart a new insecurity and fear. I don't feel safe any more and a Department of Homeland Security can't return me to the blissful ignorance I had in the years prior to September 11, 2001. The illusion of security had allowed me to live my life in a bubble, as an individual, without the awful responsibility for the rest of the people on this planet with whom I need to survive.

My illusions about God were dismantled in 2002 when the church came tumbling down, or so it seemed at the time. I realized, along with many others, that I had an idea of the church that no longer fit with what was screaming from the front-page headlines day after day. The successive scandalous revelations destroyed any remaining illusions I had. These had given me the security that religion would keep me safe, make me good and whitewash the problems around me. I learned instead that problems are within religious people themselves, including me.

Illusions protect us from the vulnerability we fear. We each have our own vulnerabilities. I know a woman who, as a child, lived with uncertainty about having a roof over her head and enough money to pay the bills. Her parents couldn't hold jobs and often, when her dad was between one job and the next, the family found themselves on the street. Now she has a job and her own family. She stresses over the bills, her job performance and the neatness of her house. This is *her* area of vulnerability, the place where she tries to create security.

Counseling might help ease some of her obsessive fear over losing her job, but the ability to hold a job and maintain a home will probably always cause her more than ordinary worry. Stressed about her job, she often works late, brings work home over the weekends, and is constantly on the lookout for better job opportunities. These behaviors give her the illusion of security: "Nothing will happen if I perform well in my job." On another level, however, she wishes she could relax and trust life. For the illusion of security, she sacrifices time with her family and opportunities to develop her love for beauty and music.

<hr>

Breaking Open Your Life

Find a quiet place for this exercise.

Write the following ten times: "I am safe in the hands of God to whom I belong." As you write, pay attention to the negative or skeptical thought that jumps into your head. Write that down, too. For example, while I am writing "I am safe in the hands of God to whom I belong" I may think, "Sure, but one nuclear or chemical attack and I'd be dead." Write that down, and go on to write again, "I am safe in the hands of God to whom I belong." After you finish, go back and read what you have written. Let the truth that you are safe in the hands of God penetrate your spirit.

<hr>

God Enters Our Fear

We are controlled by what we fear will happen. We become defenseless against that fear when we remain trapped by the need to pretend we have security, safety, or happiness. Fear dries up the wellspring of prayer. At some point in our lives, however, we realize that we do not have any real power to protect ourselves. The fragility we feel as human beings can be terrifying.

One day, however, I was looking at a manger scene and came to see that Jesus *chose* our human vulnerability. Our feeling of being vulnerable and unsafe is something that God embraced in Jesus, something he did not run away from. God understands our vulnerability because he has experienced it, and God showed us that it does not have the ultimate say in our lives.

God's vulnerability appears dramatically in the Garden of Olives, where Jesus went with his disciples after the Last Supper. When Jesus knelt in the Garden, what was racing through his mind? Did he wish he could see his mother? Did images of other trials and crucifixions he had seen invade his imagination? Did he wonder if there was a way out? Did he try to see where he had failed?

As fear gained ground, Jesus prayed desperately to his Father, the God who had refused to let his creatures be lost to death, the God who had sent his Son to show us the way to life, yet had left us free to accept or reject him. In the darkness, Jesus did as the Father had done. He emptied himself of his desires for his own life and, as the Father had done, poured out his life that we might receive life and know how to love.

That scandalous night, when human beings sold their Savior for silver, God in Jesus filled innocent suffering for all time with his presence. He himself endured the pain. When Jesus said, "Not my will but yours be done" (Lk 22:42), this was an act of vulnerability, of complete selflessness, of dependence and utter defenselessness in the face of evil. This act of love is the answer to our fear of being vulnerable. It shows, first, that the Father is present in our struggles with evil and suffering, actively helping us. Second, it shows us that we surmount evil by finding in the midst of it a way to love another.

Breaking Open Your Life

You might try this exercise in church or a place of prayer.

Return to the last exercise where you wrote, "I am safe in the hands of God to whom I belong," along with the thoughts that came as you did so. Now take the thoughts that these words provoked and turn them into an affirmation of God's love for you. For example, "It would take one nuclear or chemical attack and I'd be dead, but I am still safe in the hands of God to whom I belong." Softly repeat this new prayer of faith and security in God's love several times. Do the same for each of the phrases you wrote in the last exercise.

Letting Go

In *The Road Less Traveled*, Scott Peck wrote, "The only real security in life lies in relishing life's insecurity."[1] Your prayer will be released within you as you trust that in letting go of illusions, you discover that God and life are ultimately trustworthy. The letting go of illusions doesn't depend entirely on psychological insight, although that is helpful. Letting go of illusions is the conscious acceptance of what is happening, the decision to give yourself to others, trusting that God will show you the next step.

Sometimes we think we are doing ourselves a favor by holding on to our security, being strong, not letting others get ahead of us, pushing our weight around. However, as David

Whyte wrote in his book, *The Heart Aroused,* "Some things cannot be spoken of or discovered until we have been stuck, incapacitated, or blown off course for a while. Plain sailing is pleasant, but you are not going to explore many unknown realms that way."[2]

During times of insecurity and vulnerability we are especially susceptible to the movement of God. We are made gentle, humbled, not so sure of ourselves, and thus much more likely to experience our true selves. After enough experiences of vulnerability you may begin to realize that it is in these moments that you feel the most free. It is when you have the least to lose that you are the most secure. These moments turn down the volume of your pride, lower the static of your fear, and give you the welcome experience of who you truly are: a creature beloved of God.

We don't need to give up our security in dramatic ways—this would be unhealthy and in some cases put us or others at risk. This is not the vulnerability God asks of us in prayer. God asks us to embrace the daily insecurities—those meetings where our buttons get pushed, small but persistent character flaws we wish we didn't have, the struggle to leave the office on time at least twice a week. The opportunities are endless. They are particular to each person.

Without others noticing, you can turn to God in these moments of personal poverty. Reflect on what happened. What were you feeling? Do you know why? Offer to God whatever it is that has happened and all that you are feeling. Then talk to God as to a dear friend. Tell God your desires and offer God your love.

Breaking Open Your Life

The next time you participate in the Eucharist, unite yourself to the vulnerability of Jesus who made himself our food that in his poverty we might become rich.

Notes:

[1] M. Scott Peck, *The Road Less Traveled* (New York: Touchstone Books, 1988).
[2] David Whyte, *The Heart Aroused* (New York: Doubleday, 1994).

CHAPTER FOUR

Choosing the Way of Tenderness

And that is how I feel, always and without cease: "As if I were lying in your arms, oh God, so protected and sheltered and so steeped in eternity."

—Etty Hillesum, *An Interrupted Life: The Diaries of Etty Hillesum 1941-43*

The incessant and indiscriminate use of the word "love" has stripped it of its power. We love french fries, we love parents, we love friends, we love God, we love a sunny day, we love anything that serves or pleases us. We love everything, and, therefore, we really *love* nothing. The word no longer conveys the sense of risk, vulnerability, creative selflessness, and dispossession that accompany any authentic movement of the heart toward the other.

The word tenderness, on the other hand, makes us cringe. Tenderness is the opposite of competition, arrogance, and ruthlessness. Tenderness is risky; it draws people to the truth of who they are.

Tenderness describes what Jesus Christ has done for us.

Christ Jesus, who, though he was in the form of God, did not regard equality with God as something to be

> exploited, but emptied himself, taking the form of a slave,
> being born in human likeness. And being found in human
> form, he humbled himself and became obedient to the
> point of death—even death on a cross. Therefore God also
> highly exalted him and gave him the name that is above
> every name, so that at the name of Jesus every knee
> should bend, in heaven and on earth and under the earth,
> and every tongue should confess that Jesus Christ is
> Lord, to the glory of God the Father.
>
> PHILLIPPIANS 2:5-11

God took the risk of being rejected when he "became flesh and lived among us" (Jn 1:14). God encountered us face to face. In Christ, God spoke to us, dialogued with us, shared our feelings and our pain, saw things through our eyes, listened to us, and offered his life for ours. The way of God is the way of risk, of vulnerability, of creative selflessness, of complete dispossession. God's way is the way of tenderness.

His death on the cross was a death of irrelevance. God hung on the cross defenseless and unprotected. God died an apparent failure. This is God's way. It wasn't just a blip on the screen of God's power. This is God's power. Weakness, failure, irrelevance, helplessness. Today we often cry out as did the people who watched him die, "Show us your power. Come down from the cross! Prove to us that you really are God." We say, "If you truly exist, then save people from death, stop a hurricane, fix my problems! If you do this, I'll believe."

We want God to show us his power on our terms. We want God's show of power to protect us from vulnerability, the risk of relationships, failure, and irrelevance.

But God's way has not changed. He walks into our situations of vulnerability, he risks hearing our stories, he holds us when we fail. In return, he asks us not to run from where he has chosen to be. God has embraced our creaturehood, and gives us courage to do the same. To be creature is to be powerless. To be creature is to be *loved*. God can't be tempted to act in ways that will promote our competitiveness, our self-protective isolation from the other or our self-aggrandizement. Instead God calls us to follow his way, the divine way of tenderness, in the midst of the reality of daily life.

~~~~

Breaking Open Your Life

Take a vulnerability quiz! Finish these sentences:
My father defined failure as....
When I failed, my mother....
The first test in school that I failed was....
I am afraid to fail because....
When I hear the word "creature" I think of....
When I hear the word "power" I think of....
When I hear the word "tenderness" I think of....

~~~~

Bringing Life Out of Death

Perhaps the strongest contemporary image of this way of tenderness can be found in the film *Life Is Beautiful.* In late 1930s Italy, Guido, a Jew, meets beautiful Dora through a bizarre car and bicycle accident. Smitten, he rides his uncle's horse—which anti-Semites have painted green—into the hotel where Dora is and literally sweeps her off her feet. Soon after they marry and have a son, Giosuè.

Five years later the Nazis arrest Guido and Giosuè and ship them to a concentration camp. In order to hide the horrible reality of the camp from his son and to hide his son from the camp authorities, Guido creates a game. The first person to gain a thousand points wins a real army tank. All Giosuè has to do is to stay hidden. Guido conceals his son, and manages to bring him food and other things to keep him happy.

The movie is filled with images of tenderness in the midst of brutal realities. In a Nazi concentration camp, where human life is nearly impossible, love chooses the way of imaginative kenosis—self-emptying. Guido's choice transforms death into life and violence into tenderness.

We see acts of tenderness in the *via crucis,* the way of the cross. Jesus comforts the women. Jesus forgives the good thief. Jesus gives the care of his mother over to John. While submitting to an unjust sentence of death that brought with it excruciating suffering and humiliation, Jesus still reached out tenderly to those who suffered with him. He showed us how to be a person of mercy and hope.

Only one who has the experience of being accepted and freely loved can remain open and tender in the face of evil, rejection, denial, bitterness, hate, and despair. Only such tenderness can convince another that they are truly lovable precisely in their negative reality.

It is in prayer alone that we discover this place of tenderness in our own lives.

Jobs can be a place where we experience the pressures of competition, marginalization and injustice. Prayer is the place of tenderness which counteracts callousness, the armor we may adopt simply to survive.

Parenting can leave us little time for ourselves. Prayer is the place where we develop the tenderness to tend to our family's needs with delicacy and patience.

Pastoral ministry can burn out our heart and imagination while we care for others. Prayer is the place where we allow the Lord to tenderly attend to our own heart.

In short, prayer restores us to ourselves, and to others, and opens our heart to God.

Problems in prayer may arise when we need so much healing from our experiences in the world and with others that we are not able to risk openness with God or ourselves. Often we are not even aware that we have closed down in self-protection.

Breaking Open Your Life

Find a quiet place where you have the time and the privacy to look back over your life.

Imagine five ways you would grow if you could trust God's love for you.

Imagine five ways your relationships would improve if you were able to trust others around you.

Hold these new possibilities in your mind as you consider the following. Allow the Lord to speak to you as he spoke to this woman who sought his help.

The key to tenderness is imagination. One day as Jesus walked with his apostles a woman cried out, trying to get their attention. His apostles said, "Lord, get rid of her. She is crying out and making a disturbance." Jesus didn't follow the apostles' suggestion. Instead he turned and asked her what she wanted. Jesus imagined something different for the woman than had the apostles. They just wanted to silence this nuisance to make things better for themselves. By speaking with her, however, Jesus made something new possible for the woman.

Dreaming a New Future

The secret to changing a situation is to imagine something new.

Sometimes the only way to rise above a painful situation is to imagine a new way, a direction different from that which would make sense to others. Prayer is where we can imagine the possibility of living with joy and harmony in situations that are painful and difficult. Prayer is the place we can put our guard down, allow God's imagination to take hold of us, and respond to our future with creativity.

God dreamt of a new future for humanity and paid the price for it by taking on himself the debt we owed. We can create a new future by dreaming of the Kingdom, by imagining new ways to overcome hatred and violence with the tenderness of love.

Breaking Open Your Life

When you have some quiet time, think about a particular situation that you find difficult. What are the contributing factors? What would be your first impulse in handling this situation?

Slowly pray the hymn from the Letter to the Philippians that appears at the beginning of this chapter. Try to get in touch with the fear that might draw you away from vulnerability and the risk of relationships. Try to imagine new ways of being in this situation, ways that reflect God's determination to walk into situations of vulnerability and failure.

CHAPTER FIVE

Salvation Is God's Miracle

Love wants to reach out and manhandle us, Break all our teacup talk of God.

—Hafiz, *The Gift: Poems by Hafiz, the Great Sufi Master*

I t is hardest to choose the way of tenderness with ourselves. We are unreconciled with the darkest and most confused places within ourselves, in which we discern only wounds, faults and sins. When we open our hearts to another—friend, spiritual director, therapist—we are hoping most deeply not for reassuring explanations but acceptance. We pray that at least this other person, and ultimately God, will accept us just because we are, and continue to love us no matter what wounds we reveal to them.

The sacrament of reconciliation is the place where we can meet most directly God's acceptance, which he has definitively shown us in the life, death and resurrection of his Son. It is in the sacrament of reconciliation that we experience the exquisite tenderness of God, tending our wounds, washing, forgiving, healing. For many today, however, this experience of reconciliation with God in the community of the church has become almost nonexistent. We long to repair the most vital relationship of our lives, yet many find themselves adrift when it comes to the celebration of this sacrament.

The world has lost the sense of sin could be an explanation, and maybe that's so. Somehow I believe that, at least for some, it is the sign of a more personal struggle. A friend of mine from Tanzania was assigned to a U.S. parish and quickly realized that there were very few who availed themselves of this sacrament. He decided to make it known that he was available all day Saturday in the rectory for anybody who would like to come to talk. Before long there was a good number of individuals who came to speak with him about their situations and struggles. Through this means he gently opened the door to the possibility of the celebration of the sacrament with these individuals, allowing them to experience God's forgiveness and acceptance, allowing them to become reconciled with the darkest places of their lives and to embark on a renewed relationship with God and the church.

I believe my friend's story has much to say to Catholics in our society. We have grown much more psychologically savvy than our parents, have imbibed secular attitudes and values, and find ourselves out of breath and out of time, so that sacramental reconciliation becomes, for many, too difficult to bother with. Over twenty years ago a once-a-week confession of sins and failings became impossible for me. Each week I said the same things and heard the same words and received the same penance. One week I felt I could no longer do this and many years of struggle began as I tried desperately to understand the meaning of this sacrament in my life.

God was so gentle. Over the following thirteen years I experienced a range of feelings as I attempted to "get my hands around" the sinfulness in my life. I experienced uncertainty: "I know there is so much that is imperfect within me, but I can't pinpoint individual things." I knew there was so much in my life that was 'out of sync' with God, yet I experienced helplessness:

"My sins and failings are due mainly to the situation I am in. I feel trapped." There was also a deep sincerity: "I have this profound sense that there is something deeper that is unreconciled between God and myself, but I can't put my finger on it." And I was confused. Therapy reveals the variety of motivations behind what we do, as well as the past roots of present struggles, so I wondered how one differentiates between sin and what can be attributed to unfinished business from the past. I have discovered since that others have faced this same struggle with the mystery of salvation.

Though for thirteen years I felt I was getting nowhere in my attempts at embracing anew the sacrament of reconciliation, I believe none of that journey was a detour. God was refining my heart as I struggled to give my heart completely to him in repentance and conversion. Each person God brought into my life helped me through this journey.

God's Healing, God's Forgiveness

I remember the first time I felt understood by a confessor. The priest listened to what I had to say and responded that he had never heard anyone bring these matters to confession before. What I had brought to the sacrament of reconciliation remained, for many, nothing more than personality quirks. He suggested a book to read and encouraged me to continue as I was doing. A piece of the puzzle was put in place as I saw how constellations of everyday failings can be symptomatic of a deeper refusal to give oneself over to God completely.

Another time I brought to confession my struggle to forgive someone who had hurt me. "I can't forgive her," I remembered saying. "You *can* forgive her," the priest gently responded, "because Jesus has made it possible for you to do so. You may not be able to do so now, and you can't do it alone, but with Jesus you can." Another piece of the puzzle fell into place. Grace makes the seemingly impossible possible.

Encountering a confessor who also asked me to enumerate the places in which I had discovered God's love during the past month helped me to find a few more pieces to the puzzle that was gradually leading to a spirituality of response to God. After a retreat during which I felt that I needed to bring everything out into the open and put it on the table before God, I found a confessor who knew all the secrets of my soul but who also led me to a gentle admiration for the miracle of salvation God was working in my life. Reconciliation truly became a celebration of what God was working within me and repentance for all that, from this new vantage point, was clearly a weak and poor response to God's love. Each confession became a celebration of the newness God was bringing about.

Breaking Open Your Life

In your journal, write out the history of the sacrament of reconciliation in your life. Where does reconciliation fit into your life today?

A Deeper Response

God brings about newness in each of us. In a society where we are ranked according to our achievements or purchasing power, perhaps we have lost the serendipitous joy in the utter uniqueness of God's love for each of us shown in the very personal mission for which we are created. The response we make to this mission lifts us above binding moral norms and makes possible a free love for God, others, and ourselves. St. Maximilian Kolbe is a good example. In the midst of the violence and fear of a Nazi concentration camp, this Franciscan priest volunteered to replace in the starvation bunker a husband and father who pleaded for his life. To substitute your life for another in such circumstances is not a universally binding norm, and Kolbe would not have been sinning if he had not done so. But the newness that God was bringing about in him that day, the unique way in which he was being called to live out his discipleship to Christ, summoned him to do so. He could have resisted this sudden inspiration and not broken any commandments, but God's appeal made this decision a matter of conscience for the priest.

Responding to God's call in our conscience brings us into contact with the deepest truth of our being. This truth, we discover, is *other* than ourselves. The entire truth of the human person has its truest expression in Christ. The opening of our whole existence to the life of Christ allows us to achieve our *true* individuality. When we are entirely open to Christ, he, through his Spirit, lives out within us the mystery of his death and resurrection.

Salvation is God's miracle brought about in the heart of our freedom, molding our will to a free obedience. God's action at the very source of our moral personality unites us with a divine activity; it communicates to us a new purpose and a new will. Therefore, our Christian discipleship is not just the realization of an ideal. It demands our continuous "yes" to an activity that does not originate with us, but is, nevertheless, real in the core of our being. Rather than moralistic striving, we need to freely yield to God's activity and make no resistance to the work of the Spirit.

This yielding, this resistance, is what we bring before the Lord in the sacrament of reconciliation, because it is this relationship to God, others and ourselves that needs to be healed and given complete and total compliance. No matter how demanding this task is, in reality it is no more than compliance with the activity of God within us. Christian life is ultimately this yielding to what God is doing in us through the Spirit of Christ. It is the Spirit's activity, yet, in a mysterious way, it is also truly our own.

Moving Forward with God

We may sense this something new, this something more, but yet not know where to go with it or how to respond. We ask ourselves if what we feel most deeply within us is real. If we take the risk and step into the abyss of the promise, will God be there when we have surrendered all?

Anthony de Mello, in his book, *The Song of the Bird,* shares a reflection about someone who struggled in this way to yield to the power and promise of God:

> I had a fairly good relationship with the Lord. I would ask him for things, converse with him, praise him, thank him....
>
> But always I had this uncomfortable feeling that he wanted me to look at him. And I would not. I would talk, but look away when I sensed he was looking at me.
>
> I was afraid I should find an accusation there of some unrepented sin. I thought I should find a demand there; there would be something he wanted from me.
>
> One day I finally summoned up courage and looked! There was no accusation. There was no demand. The eyes just said, "I love you."
>
> And I walked out and, like Peter, I wept.[1]

When you want to love God more, when you wish to be all for God but are keenly aware of your weakness, then you are headed in the right direction. It seems to us to be a journey in which we reach God only at the end. But in truth God has already reached out for us and is only gathering us closer to himself. No part of your road is a detour.

Repentance is to be astounded, almost embarrassed, at the tremendous goodness shown us. It is a moment of complete honesty, the nakedness only true lovers can reverence. It is being overwhelmed by Love.

Breaking Open Your Life

Take some time to sit in a quiet, prayerful place: in a church, a favorite spot in nature, a room in your home where you will be undisturbed. Ask God to reveal to you the newness he is seeking to bring about in your life.

Note:

[1]Anthony de Mello, *The Song of the Bird* (New York: Image Doubleday, 1984).

CHAPTER SIX

Finding the Neglected Beauty of Your Life

The spiritual journey is not a success story, but a series of diminutions of the self.

—Thomas Keating, *Active Meditations for Contemplative Prayer*

What is the opposite of humility? The most obvious answer would, no doubt, be "pride." The opposite of humility, however, would more accurately be expressed as "fear": fear of God, fear of the future, fear of others, fear of death.

Fear appears in so many forms in so many lives. "I am getting old, and I am not holy. I have to get ready. I have to do something. Quick." "For me, God is out there somewhere. It's as if I wave my hands to try to get his attention when I pray. But I'm not sure he sees me." "I lived in an environment where others were always spying on me, trying to catch me not doing my work fast enough. Actually I think I am afraid that God is trying to catch me." "My son is a heroin addict. What did I do that made this happen to him?" "I see God as a judge, but I would really like to see him as a friend. But that's too much of a risk."

And the human story goes on. Since the Garden of Eden,

the sons and daughters of Adam and Eve have been afraid of God. We are afraid and so we hide. Not behind trees, but from ourselves. In doing so, we hide from God.

God Leads Us to Healing

Celine, a woman in her early forties, shared with me her struggles with sexual temptations. For over twenty years, she had felt this shame. The origin of her difficulties was lost in the shadows of the past, making it impossible to understand the genesis of her compulsion. But her struggle for freedom kept her at war with this behavior as she maintained a deep, personal, ongoing encounter with the Lord. Nevertheless, she often failed as she struggled to live a pure and upright life.

One day, when we were speaking together, she recounted a moment of grace. She had been reading the Gospel when something made her stop. In an instant, the awful realization hit her that on some level of her being she *did* want this behavior. It was easier to give in than to keep up the struggle, rationalizing that her responsibility was mitigated by whatever was at the source of her out-of-control fantasies and behavior. "I was aware that I had become a carnal person," Celine said. "It was not in the sense of neurotic guilt or shame, but just a matter-of-fact statement of my truth. Simultaneous with this realization, however, I had this profound sense of God looking upon me, holding me up with his gaze. And I was gazing at him. We were gazing into each other's eyes. And I knew that from now on it didn't matter. Even if I got rid of this and became a perfect person, it didn't matter. That's not what it is all about. The only thing that matters is that God and I continue to gaze at each other. In the end, it's not all up to me," she said. "It's about what God can do in me. And God can do everything."

Hiding from Ourselves

Why is it so hard to be truly our wounded selves with God? We unconsciously play psychological tricks on ourselves. Not ready to face our deepest wounded self, we hide it from ourselves with other, more acceptable images. I am a top-notch teacher, or a busy professional, or I am a beloved mentor others look up to. Or perhaps I am the one who knows all the ins and outs of church affairs and so don't have time to look at myself. I could be the perfect parent, or the punctual employee. Or I could be all these things put together, splitting myself into many false selves.

This gallery of ideal selves delights us and captivates us with its perfection and beauty; we find it easy to ignore the reality that gently deadens our spirit. That's why illness, failure, job loss, grief, loss of friends, can provide inroads to our deepest self, because they shatter the glitter of the idols we have created. When we have nothing left, we always have ourselves, our true selves, and buried in this true self is God, the God we have feared. We fear him because he shatters the glamour of our false selves. He does so because his love for our *true* self is so strong.

Sensing this, we stay out of reach as much as we can; we are afraid this true self will be no good. When the moment of true liberation comes, however, when we find ourselves blessed with the freedom of humility, we encounter the wonder of both ourselves and God.

It isn't necessary or helpful to try to hasten the moment of humility, because God is already working in you to bring this about. God picks up the strands of every experience of your life and weaves them together in exquisite patterns, masterfully preparing you for all that he has. Nevertheless, there are several things you can do to break open your life to God and prepare your heart for God's action.

Tips for Preparing Your Heart

First, at the end of each day, take a small notebook and jot down the positive and negative things others have said about you. Do not analyze them, just listen. Weigh what others have said to you about yourself and sift it against your own sense of inner truth. How do you feel about these statements others have made? Are you anxious? Angry? Grateful? Relieved? Write out any response you would like to make about what others have said. Do you agree? Disagree? Why? Can you give examples?

If you have a trusted friend you can share these things with, read to them both what others have said and your responses. Listen to what your friend has to say without defending or arguing. Just listen, and if appropriate ask questions. Later, when you are alone, write down your response to what your friend has said. How are you feeling? Do you agree? Disagree? Why? Choose one aspect of your personality or behavior that you would like to bring to prayer and offer to Jesus for healing.

Over time, look for patterns. Talk to God about what you perceive. If you'd like, ask someone you trust to give you honest feedback about specific areas of your life. For example, write out difficult conversations you have at work and go over these with a friend. These "verbatims" can hold important keys to seeing ourselves more accurately. If you are a parent, share with another parent how you have handled a situation and ask for feedback. Go out to breakfast with someone else at work and talk together about areas of growth they might see in you. The freedom you gain from talking with trusted friends about yourself outweighs the uncomfortable feeling of asking for feedback.

Second, at the top of a sheet of paper, write down something that upsets you. What rattles your cage? What makes you feel impatient? Frustrated? Angry? Write this down and ask yourself, "Could I say some more about this issue?" Each time you finish writing everything you have to say, challenge yourself to write more.

As you untangle your feelings, you will see beyond your

initial reaction. Each new attempt to say more about how you feel unravels aspects of your personality. Your anger at a co-worker's insolence may actually say something important about your own fear of losing your job. The demands you make on a child or student may say something important about your fear of not measuring up to your ideal of a good parent or teacher. It is important to pursue all these avenues in order to discover the fear that underlies the false self.

Finally, develop a rhythm of contemplative prayer. You do not need to be in a church or in your home to pray contemplatively. It doesn't even need to be quiet around you, although that would certainly make prayer easier. You can pray contemplatively in your car, at your desk at work, doing the laundry, running errands, watching your child's soccer game or ballet practice. Some on-the-go contemplative prayer styles:

1. Quietly repeat the Jesus Prayer: Lord Jesus Christ, have mercy on me, a sinner. Or a variation: Lord Jesus Christ, I abandon myself into your hands for all my life. Or simply pray the name of Jesus.

2. Pray the rosary reflectively.

3. Look at nature around you. Let your heart be lifted to the Creator.

4. Listen to music and let your mind quiet down and your heart center itself in God.

5. Imagine yourself in a favorite parable from the Gospels, such as the parable of the Good Shepherd, the Good Samaritan, or the Prodigal Son. Notice what Jesus does and says.

6. Picture Jesus beside you, and talk to him as to a trusted friend.

7. Pray about the situation you are in. Put your child in the hands of God while dropping her or him off at

basketball practice. Pray for the special intentions of the people stuck with you in a traffic jam. Offer a prayer before a meeting at work.

8. Read from the Bible or other book of spiritual reading during a coffee break.

Coming Home

So what is it that we find when in honest humility we come home to our real selves? Is it sin? John O'Donohue, Irish poet and Catholic scholar, believes, "There is a deep beauty hidden in the luminosity at the heart of the soul…behind the dull facade of our daily lives. Only in your solitude will you actually find it, find the neglected beauty of your life!"[1] Even if we face our wounds in finding ourselves, we discover the neglected beauty of our life.

We get so trapped in the world, in our name, our role, our relationships, our work, that our lives become boringly predictable. We become alienated even from ourselves. Our life withers from the inside out while we hunger to be seen for who we really are, to be known, to know ourselves. We need to relax, to be freed from the compulsions to "find ourselves." Our soul will find us. We discover the way to life, to the subtle movements of breath and hope, when we hand ourselves over to growth.

Celine's story wasn't finished. Four weeks after she shared her insight with me, she returned and we spoke again. She recounted that at the beginning of Mass the previous Sunday, the priest had stated during the penitential rite that Jesus had been tempted in every way that we are. It was the classic line from Hebrews (Heb 4:15), but it was as though she had heard it for the first time. A flaming sword seemed to run through her heart, and she started to cry:

> I saw that Jesus struggled with my temptations. I always imagined Jesus to be impenetrable like a slab of concrete,

deflecting the insinuations of the devil with a quote from the Old Testament. But to be tempted, you have to struggle. Feelings, desires, hopes, fears…decisions. I realized I was not alone any more. And I never would be again. I had pity on Jesus' struggle, though I know he never sinned. And Jesus has pity on me and my struggle. I have never felt so much love and somuch happiness. I can't explain it. The only thing I feel now is the wondrous miracle of being loved.

In an instant, when she came home to her true self, Celine experienced the love and transforming power of God. Sexual temptations no longer held any interest for her. They could come and go, but her desires and her attention had become riveted on One who loved her and whom she loved. Celine and the Lord were like two lovers who had discovered each other for the first time and in their love for each other were coming to know themselves anew.

Celine had handed herself over to the danger of growth. Captivated by the hand of a God who had chased her down, she discovered that the fruit of humble honesty is a new landscape of wonder.

Breaking Open Your Life

Choose one or two of suggestions in this chapter for preparing your heart for God's action and give them a try.

Note:

[1]John O'Donohue quote available at http://www.creative-edge.org/facil/odonohue.htm

CHAPTER SEVEN

The Ultimate Reliability of God

The essence of spirituality is contained in this phrase: "complete and utter abandonment to the will of God."

—Jean-Pierre de Caussade, S.J.,
Abandonment to Divine Providence

We want to know we're loved. We want to know that in spite of all our ugliness, inner poverty, and sin, we are lovable. We want to know that with all our family problems, career frustrations, and financial stress, we will be taken care of. We want to know that our sons and daughters, our spouse or parent, suffering from illness, failure, or addiction, will be healed.

We come to prayer wanting God to love us, yet holding back just in case God doesn't. We don't want to trust too much because the pain of rejection would be too great. It would affirm what we already fear about ourselves: that we aren't lovable and, in fact, even God doesn't love us. We are alone and on our own. Do we fear anything more than this cosmic loneliness?

Joseph, a friend of mine, experienced much sadness in his childhood. As a boy, he had done everything he could think of to keep his parents together, urged on by the fear of being abandoned, the ultimate devastation for a child. He knew his father had suffered from his own inner demons, but the little boy within Joseph, thirty years later, still called out for a sign of love and acceptance.

One day the Mass readings recounted the story of the two Josephs in Scripture. The first was the story of Joseph in Genesis. His brothers sold him into slavery and Joseph ended up in Egypt, the trusted right-hand man to pharaoh. Many years later, Joseph's brothers came to Egypt for food during a famine and the family, including Joseph's father, was reunited.

The second Joseph was the man chosen to be the father of Jesus on this earth, provider, sustainer, mentor, protector. My friend listened to the readings through tears of his own, not realizing at the time what was provoking his emotion. He longed for a father's acceptance, something he had never had and could not create since his father had died. With the tears, the emotional dam of thirty years of solitary living burst. Nevertheless, he still wasn't sure if he was lovable.

Talking about love brings up the problem of evil. Where is God and what is the meaning of life in the face of our pain?

Talking Your Way Through

When prayer doesn't seem to "work," when the evils in our life aren't rectified or healed, we often start another novena, light more candles, and look for miraculous prayers. We consider answers to our petitions as proof of divine love. Yet anyone who has fallen in love knows that love doesn't work like that. Two people who go into marriage with the expectation that the other will always do whatever they ask, soon make a shocking discovery about what love is not.

Love, fear, and loneliness are the most fundamental issues underlying our petitions. Prayer is the space where we assume God will show us his love. And we can't understand why miracles don't always happen. If God did love us, miracles would fix our problems, wouldn't they? And we really aren't consoled by stories of the cross, which often sound like religiously concocted excuses for God's absence or impotence.

Two people who have grown old together, either as friends or spouses, often are feeble, slow, marginalized by the young people behind them. They seem to understand each other without the need to hash out the logical meanings of what they experience. They have discovered that there is no answer to life's seemingly arbitrary ups and downs and yet, through the experience of holding hands through it all, they have experienced life's reliability. How did they reach this wisdom? It is the fruit of talking their way through life's seeming absurdity.

"Talking their way through" is how two people chase away the clouds and confusion, the terror and the tears of life's experiences. Talking your way through—you and God—is how you chase away everything that interferes with trusting the ultimate reliability of God. In prayer, this means talking to God directly about what is happening in your life. Tell God how you feel—joyful, sad, peaceful, angry, trusting, betrayed. As you tell God everything you want to say, notice how he seems to you. Does God listen? Is he close? Is he distant? Does he seem to care? Is he angry? Is he compassionate? Pay attention to what happens after you tell God what is in your heart.

Breaking Open Your Life

Begin talking things through with God by making a list of things you need to discuss with him. Choose the five most important or most urgent. Make a God-appointment in your planner for some private time for you and God. Do something nice for yourself, or something relaxing, to begin your time together. For example, bring some fresh flowers home, put on some quiet music, light a few candles, visit a church that you like, visit a park or a beach and take a long walk.

Talk to God about these five things during your appointment. Tell God how you feel, before jumping to what you want. Write down how God seems to you after you speak. Be honest. God can deal with your anger if you are upset or feel he has betrayed you. Leave at least ten minutes free after you speak for "God's time." Often while we are looking at the ocean or a sunset, listening to music or watching shadows on a wall in the silence of our home, we sense a reaction or perception within ourselves, an opening up to or awareness of God's response. Write down this new awareness.

To Believe in God's Care

To bring our woundedness and sorrows to God in prayer means more than praying novenas for relief. It is a direct encounter between the deepest places of our inner mystery with the mystery of God. Even sorrows, frustrations, anger, and hurt become bridges to a passionate intertwining with God because we now face them together, with him. The intertwining journey, however, takes place through movements toward each other and counter-movements or resistance.

Nicole always had a very formal relationship with God. She kept the rules and felt God was satisfied with her. The "romance," the passion for God that she longed for, however, seemed elusive. As the years passed, and she heard others speak of their experiences of prayer, Nicole began to feel left out.

She decided to make a retreat, hoping to develop a more satisfying relationship with God. On the first day of the retreat, the retreat director asked her to pray about the Holy Family's flight into Egypt. She was not necessarily to pray in the chapel. The director suggested she take a long walk outside and imagine herself to be on the journey with Jesus and his parents. Though at first she felt self-conscious, Nicole took her bottle of water and went out for a long walk.

She imagined herself walking beside the donkey. She listened to the conversation between Joseph and Mary. She tried to relate to their fear and anxiety as they raced away from the tiny hamlet of Bethlehem to save the life of their tiny child. She wondered what Jesus looked like as he grew up in Egypt. What were his first words? What games did he like to play? Was he excited to come to Nazareth when Joseph said it was all right to return? Thinking of times when she herself went home to visit her parents, Nicole imagined how excited Mary and Joseph must have been to see Nazareth again.

By this time Nicole was back in her room after several hours of contemplation. As she sat down on her bed, however, she became enraged and threw her water bottle against the wall. The time she had spent with the Holy Family had immersed her in the beauty of those relationships, family relationships she had never known because her parents had divorced when she was seven. Nicole shook with anger.

As she shared her pain with the retreat director over the next few days, Nicole began to talk with God for the first time about what she felt. Nicole discovered the family relationship she had with God, who had never abandoned her. Through the next six months she grew in joy, freedom, and a new sense of being loved. Her marriage began to blossom.

Then, six months later, one of her friends was diagnosed with terminal cancer and her husband was severely injured in a car accident. She visited her husband and her friend in the hospital every day, and when her husband was released took him for his physical therapy appointments. She prayed for her friend and her husband. But Nicole didn't resume the intimate relationship with God she enjoyed before her husband's accident. Her spiritual director asked her, "Do you think God has any interest in what has happened to you and your family?" For Nicole, God was employed full-time with everyone else's problems and seemed to have no time for hers.

Over the weeks Nicole shared her feelings about the accident and her friend's illness with her spiritual director, but she could not recapture the relationship with God that had begun during the retreat. God was far away. She didn't feel like praying. She had no interest in anything. She wondered what was happening.

Nicole was experiencing a counter-movement or resistance. She was being tempted against faith. God seemed not to care about her. She wasn't interested in prayer. She could barely remember the retreat that had been so full of God's presence. As she grieved over the losses she experienced, something perfectly natural, she was also experiencing the devil's efforts to disrupt her new life. He wanted her to blame this on God. The devil wanted her to get lost in his smoke screen and forget the love that she had experienced on retreat.

Without help, we are often completely unaware of this movement of resistance. Without the help of someone who sees what is really happening, we can find ourselves floating along the current the evil spirit has initiated. The evil spirit wants us to blame things on God and swim off in a sea of resentment and anger. Nicole began to behave as if the event on the retreat had never happened. It is almost a Herculean task to reach out to God at a moment such as this.

The telltale sign of the devil's action is the belief that God no longer cares, that God is distant, impotent, and aloof. Nicole's spiritual director helped her remember and reflect on her retreat experiences. As she sat with the memories, and tried to recall what she had felt, Nicole knew she had to make a decision. Eventually she knew she had to choose belief in what God had shown her on retreat, or a life of embitterment.

To believe in God's care for her meant she needed to set aside time for prayer each day. She carried a small Bible in her purse and during lunch began to read the Psalms. During her husband's appointments she read novels of other Christians who had surmounted tragedy in their lives. Little by little, Nicole was able to tell God how she felt about her sense of abandonment. And little by little, her life began once more to fall into place.

Breaking Open Your Life

Briefly write your autobiography either as a straight narrative or, if it will help the words to flow, write it in the form of a letter addressed to a trusted friend or to God. Talk about the events that have had the greatest influence on your life. Do any memories seem to be more significant? Can you write about any experiences of God's love and presence? Are you angry with God about something? Can you tell God about this? Why or why not? End your autobiography or letter by stating to God what you most desire.

Movement Two
Encountering Our Loneliness

Prayer is real when it wrestles with reality, both God's and ours. There is no event in our daily life, no matter how insignificant, that is excluded from the action of the Holy Spirit.

CHAPTER EIGHT

Prayer Is Real When It Wrestles with Reality

If you must despise life to gain it, don't forget to love it when you have gained it.

—Dietrich Bonhoeffer, *True Patriotism*

Between New Year's resolutions and Lenten resolutions, we all have engrained in our psyche the need to resolve to be better (at least twice a year). We want to change and improve our annoying personality flaws, our inappropriate character traits and our less-than-Christian behaviors. The most direct route to transformation would seem to be to discover the virtue one lacks and start praying for it. It is exactly this prayer, however, that can create quicksand in a Christian's heart.

What happens when, regardless of the months or years of prayer, you are still struggling with the same problem behavior? Is prayer to blame? Is God to blame? Are you to blame?

Clare worked in a large shop with five other employees. She told me that she knew she had to be more patient. But she felt frustrated when others snickered at her values, when decisions were made that put money before people, or when pictures of Jesus were removed from her workspace. She tried to give the others the benefit of the doubt since she didn't know their intentions. *How could she judge?* she asked herself. So Clare struggled to be more patient. When I asked if her efforts were working, she replied sheepishly, "Well, I think I'm better than I was before."

What did God want of Clare? First of all, he didn't want a perfectly patient Clare. He wanted Clare herself. By praying for patience she was in a very subtle way withholding herself from God.

By bringing before God exactly how she felt in that work situation, Clare could have brought herself to God. She could have opened herself to what God wanted to be and do in her. She felt alone, hurt, and isolated. She was frustrated at working in a place that contradicted the values on which she had built her life, a place that ran counter to the deepest desires of her soul. She had come to believe that patience meant not noticing or caring about what was happening; all she could do was go about her own life.

How did she know, however, that God didn't want her to rage about the injustices that were occurring in the name of corporate allegiance? How did she know that God didn't want her to reach out in acts of kindness toward those who were making her life difficult? The struggle and pain in Clare's heart became evident as she realized she hadn't even been able to pray for these people.

Prayer is real when it wrestles with reality, both God's and ours. There is no event in daily life, no matter how insignificant, that is excluded from the action of the Holy Spirit.

The Not-So-Perfect Jacob

> The same night [Jacob] got up and took his two wives, his two maids, and his eleven children, and crossed the ford of the Jabbok. He took them and sent them across the stream, and likewise everything that he had.

> Jacob was left alone; and a man wrestled with him until daybreak. When the man saw that he did not prevail against Jacob, he struck him on the hip socket; and Jacob's hip was put out of joint as he wrestled with him. Then he said, "Let me go, for the day is breaking." But Jacob said, "I will not let you go, unless you bless me." So he said to him, "What is your name?" And he said, "Jacob."
>
> Then the man said, "You shall no longer be called Jacob, but Israel, for you have striven with God and with humans, and have prevailed." Then Jacob asked him, "Please tell me your name." But he said, "Why is it that you ask my name?" And there he blessed him.
>
> So Jacob called the place Peniel, saying, "For I have seen God face to face, and yet my life is preserved." The sun rose upon him as he passed Penuel, limping because of his hip. Therefore to this day the Israelites do not eat the thigh muscle that is on the hip socket, because he struck Jacob on the hip socket at the thigh muscle.
>
> GENESIS 32:22-32

Still Real, Still Wrestling

Jacob saw God face-to-face, a privilege given only to great leaders in the ancient lineage of Israel. Yet Jacob was a thief and a trickster, a very capable man who was also capable of engineering things so that he got ahead. Yet God chose to encounter this man and to show him God's face. In fact, even as Jacob had fled Esau barely escaping with his life, Yahweh had appeared to him in a dream, promising to give him the land upon which he was sleeping and to make his descendants as plentiful as the dust on the ground. "I am with you and will keep you wherever you go…I will not leave you until I have done what I have promised you" (Gn 28:15).

Despite all the promises, however, Jacob still had to face his past, himself, and his brother Esau waiting for him on the other side of the river. God does not take away our reality even when we encounter him in a profound way. I suggested to Clare that we still have to wrestle with relationships, fears, hurts, guilt, desires, frustration. We even have to wrestle with God. In the wrestling, not in our perfection, is our salvation.

Psalm 73

A psalm for those who are wrestling

> Truly God is good to the upright,
>> to those who are pure in heart.
> But as for me, my feet had almost stumbled;
>> my steps had nearly slipped.
> For I was envious of the arrogant;
>> I saw the prosperity of the wicked.
>
> For they have no pain;
>> their bodies are sound and sleek.
> They are not in trouble as others are;
>> they are not plagued like other people…
>
> And they say, "How can God know?
>> Is there knowledge in the Most High?"
> Such are the wicked;
>> always at ease, they increase in riches.
> All in vain I have kept my heart clean
>> and washed my hands in innocence….
>
> When my soul was embittered,
>> when I was pricked in heart,
> I was stupid and ignorant;
>> I was like a brute beast toward you.
> Nevertheless I am continually with you;
>> you hold my right hand.
> You guide me with your counsel,
>> and afterward you will receive me with honor.
> Whom have I in heaven but you?
>> And there is nothing on earth that I desire other than
>>> you.
> My flesh and my heart may fail,
>> but God is the strength of my heart and my portion
>>> forever. (vv. 1-5, 11-13, 21-26)

Breaking Open Your Life

Take some quiet time for this exercise. The "wrestling" might take several days so give it time.

Spend prolonged time contemplating the impulses, hopes, desires, and fears of your heart. Don't try to understand, fix, or improve what you find; contemplate what is there. What might God want to do in you? Is there a situation in your life similar to Clare's dilemma? Have you made resolutions to improve? Are the resolutions working? God wants you to wrestle with him over this, and God wants you to wrestle with your past, with yourself, with others. God wants you to bring all your woundedness to him, that he might heal you in his way.

CHAPTER NINE

Prayer Is About Transformation

Oh, how sweet your presence is for me, for you are the highest good. I want to approach you in silence and seek to discover your foot-prints, that you may be pleased to unite me to yourself in marriage.

—St. John of the Cross as quoted by Edith Stein, *The Science of the Cross*

In today's culture, the spiritual has acquired a psychological meaning. In the popular imagination, it is identified with the mind or with feelings. When we feel spiritual, we think we have deep insights. When we pray, we expect to feel moved. Spirituality thus conceived is a trap. A person with high ideals or great sentiments is not necessarily more spiritual than one who neither thinks great thoughts nor feels great emotion.

Karl was forty-two, single, and depressed. He struggled through several years of therapy. Afterwards, he found mean-ing and relief in prayer. He told me, however, that he swung back and forth between feeling that all he needed to do was keep praying, and feeling that praying did nothing at all. I had the feeling that Karl thought of God as static or immobile, not interactive or interested in Karl's life. Karl's sense of God's power had been reduced to the powerlessness Karl felt within himself.

Prayer puts us in contact with a God who interacts with us, often in abrupt ways. If God seems to be letting us alone, then we should wonder if we know God as he is, or simply know a God of our own making.

The Immensity of What Is Promised

> Meanwhile Saul, still breathing threats and murder against the disciples of the Lord, went to the high priest and asked him for letters to the synagogues at Damascus, so that if he found any who belonged to the Way, men or women, he might bring them bound to Jerusalem.
>
> Now as he was going along and approaching Damascus, suddenly a light from heaven flashed around him. He fell to the ground and heard a voice saying to him, "Saul, Saul, why do you persecute me?" He asked, "Who are you, Lord?" The reply came, "I am Jesus, whom you are persecuting. But get up and enter the city, and you will be told what you are to do." The men who were traveling with him stood speechless because they heard the voice but saw no one.
>
> Saul got up from the ground, and though his eyes were open, he could see nothing; so they led him by the hand and brought him into Damascus. For three days he was without sight, and neither ate nor drank.
>
> ACTS 9:1-9

The God of the apostle Paul was a God of often dramatic interaction. This God sought people out, stopped them in their tracks, turned their lives upside down. Paul had encountered this God on the road to Damascus, where he had intended to imprison the early followers of Jesus. No horse is mentioned in the Acts of the Apostles, but artists have often depicted Paul falling from a horse as he encounters Jesus. The horse is a symbol of pride, authority, independence and control.

Struck blind, Paul learned that God had vindicated Jesus, which meant that the end times, promised in the ancient prophecies of the Hebrew Scriptures, had begun. Paul realized that the resurrection of Jesus identified Jesus as the true Messiah (Rom 1:4). Paul's zeal had been misplaced. He had no choice but to join the cause of the very ones he had been persecuting.

Instead of entering into Damascus with a battle plan, as he had intended, Paul had to enter holding someone's hand. To believe, he first had to walk through the darkness, he first had to become a child, he first had to learn what it is to be taught by God.

This encounter with Jesus did not just change Paul's way of doing things. It changed his whole being. He wrote in his letter to the first Christian community in Galatia, "It is no longer I who live, but it is Christ who lives in me" (Gal 2:20).

Ten years passed before the community of those who believed in Jesus fully accepted Paul; during that time he encountered their rejection and distrust. But his burning love for Christ helped him overcome the difficulties he faced, and led him on far-reaching missionary travels to proclaim Jesus Christ and to facilitate the acceptance of the Gentiles into the Christian community.

The Church has preserved in the New Testament the letters Paul wrote to Christian communities, most of which he himself founded: Galatia, Corinth, Philippi, Thessalonica. Though we still read his letters in the Liturgy of the Word, few lectors grasp the fire and the passion, the anger and the love, with which Paul must have written them.

Paul wrote to the Ephesians:

> I pray that the God of our Lord Jesus Christ, the Father of glory, may give you a spirit of wisdom and revelation as you come to know him, so that, with the eyes of your heart enlightened, you may know what is the hope to which he has called you, what are the riches of his glorious inheritance among the saints, and what is the immeasurable greatness of his power for us who believe, according to the working of his great power. God put this power

> to work in Christ when he raised him from the dead and
> seated him at his right hand in the heavenly places, far
> above all rule and authority and power and dominion, and
> above every name that is named, not only in this age but
> also in the age to come.
>
> EPHESIANS 1:17-21

Since the very beginning, Paul's long sentences filled with theological nuggets have been famous. They take much time and reflection to unpack. Paul is saying to the Ephesians that God uses with us the same power that he used in raising Christ from the dead, in seating Christ at his right hand in dominion over every other name in heaven and on earth, in this age and the age to come. The immeasurable greatness of his power for us who believe is the same power that brought about the turn of the ages and triumph over evil.

Spirituality is not about what we feel or even what we think. It's about ecstasy, admiration of God, and transformation. All of these can occur even when we feel devoid of any attraction or consolation. Spirituality is about placing ourselves before God in hope, trusting in the immensity of his power which will raise us from the dead.

I invited Karl to leave behind an entertainment or achievement model of prayer and embrace one of power. He needed to continue to seek psychological wholeness, and he needed to present himself before the Lord for transformation and resurrection.

Psalm 95

A celebration of God's power.

> O come, let us sing to the LORD;
>> let us make a joyful noise to the rock of our salvation!
> Let us come into his presence with thanksgiving;
>> let us make a joyful noise to him with songs of praise!

For the LORD is a great God,
  and a great King above all gods.
In his hand are the depths of the earth;
  the heights of the mountains are his also.
The sea is his, for he made it,
  and the dry land, which his hands have formed.

O come, let us worship and bow down,
  let us kneel before the LORD, our Maker!
For he is our God,
  and we are the people of his pasture,
  and the sheep of his hand.

O that today you would listen to his voice! (vv. 1-7)

Breaking Open Your Life

Try this exercise of transformative prayer.

Do you find yourself restless when you pray? Are you waiting for something to happen? Something is happening, by the very fact that God is God, and you are seeking to encounter him. Can you turn off the TV mode of praying, and instead of looking at God, allow God to look at you, to encompass you in his power, to do with you and in you what he wills? You will find "the eyes of your heart enlightened, [so that] you may know what is the hope to which he has called you, what are the riches of his glorious inheritance among the saints" (Eph 1:18).

CHAPTER TEN

Prayer Is a Direct Encounter with the Mystery of God

O burning Mountain, O chosen Sun, O perfect Moon, O fathomless Well, O unattainable Height, O Clearness beyond measure, O Wisdom without end, O Mercy without limit, O Strength beyond resistance, O Crown beyond all majesty: The humblest thing you created sings your praise.

—Mechthild of Magdeburg, as quoted in *The Worshipping Church: A Hymnal*

Jolene, an older woman, was sharing with me about her prayer. She was concerned because nothing seemed to be happening. "I read a passage from Scripture," she said, "but then I wonder what else I should be doing." Jolene had read about different ways of praying with Scripture, but nothing seemed to help.

As we spoke, I prayed for God to show us what he was doing in her life. It was then that I realized that we had been trying to learn new ways of praying with Scripture instead of looking for what God was doing in her life already. We needed to break open the "scriptures" of her life, and observe the word God was speaking *in* her.

Prayer is about listening before it is about communicating. Often, communication in our everyday life is about us getting *our* point across. This habit carries over into prayer. Prayer becomes a one-way stream of words and expectations. We are not accustomed to listening to others, and this is especially difficult when the Other is unseen.

God speaks to us, however, from the midst of our human reality, a pattern of communication God established in the garden of Eden and brought to a climax in the Incarnation. God's word to us could be as simple as a phrase that jumps out of a book we are reading, a scene from a movie that moves us to see God or our situation in a new way, an unexpected e-mail from a friend.

A Woman Who Listened

In the sixth month the angel Gabriel was sent by God to a town in Galilee called Nazareth, to a virgin engaged to a man whose name was Joseph, of the house of David. The virgin's name was Mary. And he came to her and said, "Greetings, favored one! The Lord is with you." But she was much perplexed by his words and pondered what sort of greeting this might be.

The angel said to her, "Do not be afraid, Mary, for you have found favor with God. And now, you will conceive in your womb and bear a son, and you will name him Jesus. He will be great, and will be called the Son of the Most High, and the Lord God will give to him the throne of his ancestor David. He will reign over the house of Jacob forever, and of his kingdom there will be no end."

Mary said to the angel, "How can this be, since I am a virgin?" The angel said to her, "The Holy Spirit will come upon you, and the power of the Most High will overshadow you; therefore the child to be born will be holy; he will be called Son of God...."

Then Mary said, "Here am I, the servant of the Lord; let it be with me according to your word." Then the angel departed from her.

LUKE 1:26-38

Influenced by the work of artists, we are accustomed to picturing the angel speaking to Mary when she was at prayer. Scripture, however, is silent about what Mary was doing when the visitor from God arrived.

Noel Rowe's poem, *Magnificat*, pictures Mary in the kitchen, peeling vegetables, listening to children playing outside with their dog. Silence fluttered into the room with a breeze. God had captured her attention while she was occupied with her daily work, had surprised her in her daily round. This is the way God communicates. He surprises us, catches us off guard, so that he can get his word in first.

There are times when I feel knocked off my feet by what God has said. The answer then is always yes, it may be a struggling yes, but nevertheless it is a grasping for the beauty that has already claimed us for eternity.

These are the "scriptures" of our lives. These are the moments we must read. These are the words we must hear. When we take these revelations to prayer, we will find we resonate with these images, inspirations, and direction. Each new reading reaches deeper and deeper into our heart and transforms our life.

Breaking Open Your Life

Remember a moment you experienced sudden, unexpected, spiritual peace. Relive the experience and try to notice what God was doing within you, what God *is* doing even now.

Risking the Encounter with God

One evening, I spoke to a mentor about a long-standing difficulty in my life that left me wounded and broken. After we explored it briefly, she asked if I had ever talked to God about it in prayer. I had to admit I hadn't. Talking to a spiritual director was the closest to God that I had ever come with this brokenness. I could not remember even one time that I had prayed about it in the previous twenty years.

When we bring our woundedness to God in prayer, the deepest parts of our inner mystery encounter the mystery of God. It's like the relationship between lovers. One couple might be on good terms because they never speak honestly to each other. But lovers who are determined to be united share every inch of their lives. So it is with our relationship with God. As we share our sorrows, frustrations, anger, and hurt, these become bridges to a passionate intertwining because we face them together.

A Courageous Woman

One of the Pharisees asked Jesus to eat with him, and he went into the Pharisee's house and took his place at the table.

And a woman in the city, who was a sinner, having learned that he was eating in the Pharisee's house, brought an alabaster jar of ointment. She stood behind him at his feet, weeping, and began to bathe his feet with her tears and to dry them with her hair. Then she continued kissing his feet and anointing them with the ointment....

Turning toward the woman, he said to Simon, "Do you see this woman? I entered your house; you gave me no water for my feet, but she has bathed my feet with her tears and dried them with her hair. You gave me no kiss, but from the time I came in she has not stopped kissing my feet. You did not anoint my head with oil, but she has anointed my feet with ointment.

> Therefore, I tell you, her sins, which were many, have been forgiven; hence she has shown great love. But the one to whom little is forgiven, loves little." Then he said to her, "Your sins are forgiven…go in peace."
>
> LUKE 7:36-38, 44-48

It was a risk to bring to Jesus the wounds that marred so much of my life. I had to discover the child I was more than thirty years ago, and allow that child to encounter God. I didn't think that I could do this. It was difficult reconnecting with the little girl within. But I had prepared for this new encounter through many years of counseling and much personal work. This was the beginning of truly understanding what love is, the love for which I had thirsted.

Psalm 103

A prayer of someone willing to risk an encounter with God.

> Bless the LORD, O my soul,
>> and all that is within me,
>> bless his holy name.
> Bless the LORD, O my soul,
>> and do not forget all his benefits—
> who forgives all your iniquity,
>> who heals all your diseases,
> who redeems your life from the Pit,
>> who crowns you with steadfast love and mercy,
> who satisfies you with good as long as you live
>> so that your youth is renewed like the eagle's.
>
> The LORD works vindication
>> and justice for all who are oppressed…
>
> For as the heavens are high above the earth,
>> so great is his steadfast love toward those who fear
>>> him;
> as far as the east is from the west,
>> so far he removes our transgressions from us.

As a father has compassion for his children,
> so the LORD has compassion for those who fear him.
For he knows how we were made;
> he remembers that we are dust. (vv. 1-6, 11-14)

Breaking Open Your Life

Take time to reflect on how it is with your soul. What has been your experience of growth and maturity? How have you grown through the celebration of the liturgy and the sacraments and through prayer? What have you gained from counseling, self-help books, or good advice from a friend? Is there a part of your life that you haven't brought to prayer yet? What might happen if you did? If you are not ready, be gentle with yourself. The Holy Spirit will bring this to mind when it is the right time for you.

CHAPTER ELEVEN

Prayer Is Difficult When You Are Running Away

Dance, when you're broken open. Dance, if you've torn the bandage off. Dance in the middle of the fighting. Dance in your blood. Dance, when you're perfectly free.

—Jaluddin Rumi, *The Essential Rumi*

I once spent an evening with a Vietnamese friend, a priest who would be returning shortly to his own country. We had been students together and had recently graduated. We celebrated the end of studies and the joy of friendship at a small family-style restaurant. In the midst of the hurrying waitresses and the children running from table to table, our conversation quickly turned to something that was on his mind.

"I don't know what's wrong," Fr. Chris began. "I used to pray all the time—in my family and in the seminary in Vietnam. Now I can't pray. I end up watching TV. I feel closer to God when I am holding the hands of people who are dying in the hospital where I am a chaplain than when I sit down to pray. I don't feel anything anymore."

Later in the conversation Chris shared his dilemma about returning to Vietnam. He could return immediately or wait a year, pursue his preparation for teaching, and return with friends who would be going back. Although others were expecting him to return immediately, he had good reason to hesitate. Coming to America, learning a new language and studying in a country other than his own, had been a "death and resurrection" experience for him. Returning to Vietnam would be another "death" experience, and he wasn't sure if he was up to it. "On the other hand," he stated, "if I bring God into the picture I know God would want me to go back immediately."

As Chris weighed the alternatives, I listened. When he asked my opinion, I told him that I thought he wasn't ready to make a decision yet.

What If God Doesn't Expect Anything from Us?

Jesus is often portrayed in the Gospels as making decisions. More often than not, the decisions he makes shock either someone in the narrative or us.

> At that time Jesus went through the grainfields on the sabbath; his disciples were hungry, and they began to pluck heads of grain and to eat. When the Pharisees saw it, they said to him, "Look, your disciples are doing what is not lawful to do on the sabbath." He said to them, "Have you not read what David did when he and his companions were hungry? He entered the house of God and ate the bread of the Presence, which it was not lawful for him or his companions to eat, but only for the priests. Or have you not read in the law that on the sabbath the priests in the temple break the sabbath and yet are guiltless? I tell you, something greater than the temple is here. But if you had known what this means, 'I desire mercy and not sacrifice,' you would not have condemned the guiltless."
>
> MATTHEW 12:1-7

We often believe, as Chris did, that God would want us to do the hardest thing so as to prove our love for him. Anything that took into account various aspects of our situation would certainly be selfish. However, if we look at this account of Matthew,

Jesus takes into account his disciples' hunger. He allows them to do what was forbidden on the Sabbath. Jesus was merciful, revealing to us the face of God, "the Merciful One."

In his book *Fire of Mercy, Heart of the World*, Erasmo Leiva-Merikakis, writes:

> Such mercy does not rest for Christians on a basis of sentiment. It is the spontaneous, creative movement of life-bestowing love that bends down where it detects misery. Hence the word *misericordia* in Latin, the movement of the "heart" (*cor*) that is shaken at the sight of the other's plight (*miseria*) and moves to do something, going out of itself and toward the other. It is the active love of God that wants to fill every void and darkness in the human heart with life and joy.[1]

Because Chris was afraid God would insist that he return to Vietnam immediately, putting his life and his vocation in danger, he couldn't and didn't pray. He avoided God's gaze because he thought he knew what God was like. He believed that God looked at him as a master eyes his slave, using him at whim.

God loves us, certainly, Chris knew, but it was not with the love of mercy and compassion. It was a strict love, without reference to the law of growth and the nuances of a situation. This skewed perception of God distorted Chris' sense of what God might want in his regard. Therefore, I urged him not to make an immediate decision on the erroneous assumption that God always wanted us to make the choice that was hardest and most unpleasant. Instead, I suggested he return to prayer and ask God to reveal himself and his love to him.

Psalm 126

A psalm of one who has discovered God's compassion.

> When the LORD restored the fortunes of Zion,
>   we were like those who dream.
> Then our mouth was filled with laughter,
>   and our tongue with shouts of joy;

then it was said among the nations,
    "The LORD has done great things for them."
The LORD has done great things for us,
    and we rejoiced.

Restore our fortunes, O LORD,
    like the watercourses in the Negeb.
May those who sow in tears
    reap with shouts of joy.
Those who go out weeping,
    bearing the seed for sowing,
shall come home with shouts of joy,
    carrying their sheaves.

Breaking Open Your Life

Sometimes we assume God couldn't be as pleased with us as he is with others because we don't spend hours in prayer, haven't given our life to God as a priest or religious, aren't able to avoid sinful habits, or haven't given up everything to live with the poor. All of us have our own personal litany of why God couldn't love us. What if God didn't expect anything from you as a sign of love, anything other than allowing God to love you? How would your life change?

Note:

[1]Erasmo Leiva-Merikakis, *Fire of Mercy, Heart of the World* (San Francisco: Ignatius, 1996), p. 197.

CHAPTER TWELVE

Prayer Brings Us Further into Silence

*Silence is God's first language; everything else is a poor transla-
tion. In order to hear that language, we must learn to be still and
to rest in God.*

—Thomas Keating, *Invitation to Love*

When I was a little girl, I wanted to be a contemplative
sister. I still respect the cloistered life though I know that this is
not the vocation to which I have been called. Nevertheless, I
have loved silence and solitude since I entered the convent.
Prayer requires a certain silence and solitude and prayer leads
us further into that quiet place.

The cloistered life looks very tempting to many of us in
this noisy world. Sometimes we are so far removed from any
experience of real silence that we don't know the peace it can
create for us. At times, despite our longing for solitude, our
work or family obligations make it impossible to remove
ourselves from other's company.

Come and Rest Awhile

> The apostles gathered around Jesus, and told him all
> that they had done and taught. He said to them, "Come
> away to a deserted place all by yourselves and rest a
> while." For many were coming and going, and they had
> no leisure even to eat. And they went away in the boat
> to a deserted place by themselves.
>
> Now many saw them going and recognized
> them, and they hurried there on foot from all the towns
> and arrived ahead of them. As he went ashore, he saw
> a great crowd; and he had compassion for them,
> because they were like sheep without a shepherd; and
> he began to teach them many things.
>
> MARK 6:30-34

Sometimes I wonder why Jesus said, "Let's get out of here and
go to a deserted place so that we can rest a while." Did he feel
harassed? Did he feel compassion for the apostles who were
tired? Did he feel a bit mischievous as he tried to slip away? No
matter how he felt, throughout the Gospels the evangelists
record him regularly planning his getaways. Most often they
were at night, while others slept. Then he and the Father would
have their time alone together.

Though my daily schedule includes time to get away for
silence and solitude, I realize that even in solitude I am not truly
alone. I bring with me my dreams, opinions, desires, expectations, thoughts, fears, curiosities and judgments. The quiet
hours are marred by the screaming within me.

I once had a conversation with a good friend. I was
becoming very anxious about several sets of circumstances—
political, diocesan, communitarian. He himself cared deeply
about these situations and felt a certain responsibility
regarding them.

He shared with me some very good advice. "If you become agitated, your efforts to address any of these problems will be doomed from the start. Anxious feelings are not bad, it is just that we need to hold these anxious feelings in a larger vessel of hope. It is the one with a dream who can lead others into a new future."

I realize now that the more we pray, the more we will experience a deeper silence, so that eventually we will be able to turn to those who ask for our time and attention as Jesus did: "As [Jesus] went ashore, he saw a great crowd; and he had compassion for them" (Mk 6:34).

Psalm 131

The prayer of one waiting on the dream.

> O LORD, my heart is not lifted up,
>   my eyes are not raised too high;
> I do not occupy myself with things
>   too great and too marvelous for me.
> But I have calmed and quieted my soul,
>   like a weaned child with its mother;
>   my soul is like the weaned child that is with me.
>
> O Israel, hope in the LORD
>   from this time on and forevermore.

Breaking Open Your Life

Take some moments to contemplate your heart as you go through your day. Where do you most feel a desire for silence or a vacation? Are you able to create a mini-vacation at those times? Insert solitude breaks into your day and see how that affects your life.

Jesus was concerned because his apostles didn't even have time to eat. What would his concern be for you? He says also to you, "Come apart and rest a while in my arms. I will feed you, I will console you, I will strengthen you, I will give you rest."

Tuning into Chaos

Sometimes, before we enter into the silence we've been speaking of, we need to tune into the chaos in our hearts. Books and presentations on prayer often expound on the tremendous peace prayer brings, and rightly so. Prayer can bring us to reconciliation with God and ourselves; in prayer we can more easily make decisions we won't regret; in prayer we can sense the direction in which God is leading us and the movement of our own desires; in prayer we open to God's life growing in us. But prayer many times brings us through the dark chaos of our lives before we arrive at peace. A woman with clinical depression once told me that she believed that she should be able to control her messy emotions with positive thoughts. I asked her, "Could it be possible, instead, that God is speaking to you somehow *in* the emotional turmoil you have been experiencing?" Our emotions, though powerful and messy, can signal to us the Spirit's work.

Sometimes Even Tears Save

Now Peter was sitting outside in the courtyard. A servant-girl came to him and said, "You also were with Jesus the Galilean." But he denied it before all of them, saying, "I do not know what you are talking about." When he went out to the porch, another servant-girl saw him, and she said to the bystanders, "This man was with Jesus of Nazareth." Again he denied it with an oath, "I do not know the man."

> After a little while the bystanders came up and said to Peter, "Certainly you are also one of them, for your accent betrays you." Then he began to curse, and he swore an oath, "I do not know the man!" At that moment the cock crowed. Then Peter remembered what Jesus had said: "Before the cock crows, you will deny me three times." And he went out and wept bitterly.
>
> MATTHEW 26:69-75

Peter's bitter tears, his utter remorse, catapulted him no doubt into intense regret. The last words Peter spoke about Jesus during Jesus' life were words of denial. He had no idea on that inconsolable night that he would ever see Jesus alive again. Jesus would be executed, but even worse, Peter had directly denied him, denied having even known him.

If Peter had tried to control his chaotic emotions, he would never have penetrated the sorrow he felt and discovered the immense love he bore for Jesus. This love was so immense that when John recognized Jesus on the shore after the resurrection, Peter instantly "put on some clothes…and jumped into the sea" (Jn 21:7).

Peter reached the truth through deep sorrow over his betrayal of the Lord. He was ready for the Lord to remake him into someone who relied not on his own strength, but on the tender goodness of the One who loved him. Jesus asked Peter three times if he loved him, but only after he showed Peter that he was loved already. When we reach the impossibility of authentic love, we discover that our love is made possible by the One who is Love, the One who loved us long before we were born.

Psalm 6

A psalm for one experiencing a roller coaster of emotions

O LORD, do not rebuke me in your anger,
    or discipline me in your wrath.
Be gracious to me, O LORD, for I am languishing;
    O LORD, heal me, for my bones are shaking with terror.
My soul also is struck with terror,
    while you, O LORD—how long?

Turn, O LORD, save my life;
    deliver me for the sake of your steadfast love.
For in death there is no remembrance of you;
    in Sheol who can give you praise?

I am weary with my moaning;
    every night I flood my bed with tears;
    I drench my couch with my weeping.
My eyes waste away because of grief;
    they grow weak because of all my foes.

Depart from me, all you workers of evil,
    for the LORD has heard the sound of my weeping.
The LORD has heard my supplication;
    the LORD accepts my prayer.
All my enemies shall be ashamed and struck with terror;
    they shall turn back, and in a moment be put to shame.

Breaking Open Your Life

In a quiet place, or with a friend, allow yourself time to think over these questions.

Do you have any uncried tears, unexpressed rage, unacknowledged sorrow? Are you holding a stiff upper lip, going through life unwilling to bend under the weight of pain? God is found even in the deepest corner of your darkness. God waits for you there. He is leading you to look into the sorrow and grasp for his hands and his love.

CHAPTER THIRTEEN

Prayer Is Not a Goal But a Process

If sometimes he strays a bit from that divine presence, God makes Himself felt in his soul to recall it to Him, often when he is engaged in his regular duties; he responds with strict fidelity to these interior entreaties.... And then it seems to him that this God of love, satisfied with these few words, returns and rests again in the very depths of his soul.

—Brother Lawrence of the Resurrection, *The Practice of the Presence of God*

P rayer is like school. If we don't attend classes, we don't learn. If we don't do the readings and the homework, we don't grow. Prayer is not an ideal to attain, it's a process we undergo.

Just as a teacher watches how students digest the material, making sure they understand the concepts correctly, prayer also demands some kind of mentorship. It is easy to mistake the first thought that crosses our mind for God's voice, or to try out every new idea that comes our way. Prayer, instead, integrates the surprising and free dynamic of the Spirit so that we grow according to our creaturehood.

Jamie, a young student, told me about his struggle with prayer. He didn't feel that God was there when he prayed so instead he jogged, watched TV, and visited friends. Though he felt a longing for something deeper in his life, prayer remained impossible. Whole months separated the times he attempted to pray.

We Need Others in the Spiritual Life

> After some time had passed, the Jews plotted to kill [Saul], but their plot became known to Saul. They were watching the gates day and night so that they might kill him; but his disciples took him by night and let him down through an opening in the wall, lowering him in a basket.
>
> When he had come to Jerusalem, he attempted to join the disciples; and they were all afraid of him, for they did not believe that he was a disciple. But Barnabas took him, brought him to the apostles, and described for them how on the road he had seen the Lord, who had spoken to him, and how in Damascus he had spoken boldly in the name of Jesus.
>
> So he went in and out among them in Jerusalem, speaking boldly in the name of the Lord. He spoke and argued with the Hellenists; but they were attempting to kill him. When the believers learned of it, they brought him down to Caesarea and sent him off to Tarsus.
>
> ACTS 9:23-30

On the road to Damascus, Paul experienced an encounter with Jesus of earth-shattering proportions. He would never be the same. He immediately told others about it. He spoke about the Lord and argued with others, so much so that his life was in danger. The disciples secretly sent him out of the city. In Jerusalem, the Christians were understandably concerned about accepting a former "terrorist" into their ranks. It was Barnabas who stepped in and smoothed the way for the greatest apostle the church would ever know. Barnabas told the other apostles the story of Paul's encounter with Jesus. Could you imagine the surprise of the believers in Jerusalem when they heard Jesus was making personal appearances? And to people not of their number?

Nevertheless Paul, still a bit too argumentative, needed to be sent off to Tarsus fearing for his life. It was Barnabas who brought him back into the community after Paul spent years in his native town (Acts 11:22-26).

When Paul came back he was a changed man. He had learned that Christianity is not about the triumph of someone's ideas, but about becoming Christ. And in fact, Antioch was the first place in which the followers of Christ were called Christians (Acts 11:26).

A healthy spiritual life begins with others in the community of Christians. Like Paul, we walk a path accompanied by others. If we are venturing alone we run great risks, and the greatest of these risks is never getting started in the first place.

Jamie needed the support and guidance of a Barnabas. Someone who would turn off the TV, a friend who would pray with him, a prayer group that met regularly, or a spiritual director who would guide him through the pitfalls, obstacles and illusions of the spiritual life. If Jamie didn't show up for "class," he wouldn't learn. If he didn't show up somewhere for prayer, he wouldn't pray.

Psalm 63

A "Barnabas" psalm for someone who needs help praying.

> O God, you are my God, I seek you,
> > my soul thirsts for you;
> my flesh faints for you,
> > as in a dry and weary land where there is no water.
> So I have looked upon you in the sanctuary,
> > beholding your power and glory.
> Because your steadfast love is better than life,
> > my lips will praise you.
> So I will bless you as long as I live;
> > I will lift up my hands and call on your name.
>
> My soul is satisfied as with a rich feast,
> > and my mouth praises you with joyful lips

when I think of you on my bed,
and meditate on you in the watches of the night;
for you have been my help,
and in the shadow of your wings I sing for joy.
My soul clings to you;
your right hand upholds me. (vv. 1-8)

Breaking Open Your Life

These are good questions to discuss with a spiritual director.

What is the rhythm of prayer you have created for yourself? How does it feel to you? Are you satisfied with it? Do you want something more?

Do you have questions about prayer, the spiritual life, God? Do you feel as Jamie did, that you can't seem to get going? Or do you seem to retrace the same part of the road over and over?

Ask God what he desires for you.

God Draws Near

Dean was active in his parish and nearly every day attended the parish's early Mass.

Though he had practiced his faith for all his life and considered himself a religious person, he told me he felt he couldn't pray. Prayer for him meant mental concentration on God. Since his wayward thoughts often distracted him, he had given up hope of ever *really* praying. Dean believed that if he could control his thoughts and feelings he would be a holier person. He, like so many today, had equated mental control with holiness and prayer. He was lost in his own subjectivity in an elusive search for God.

One Christmas, during midnight Mass, Dean was deeply moved by the homily and the music. He had an indescribable feeling of warmth and belonging. Later, he mentioned this experience to me. In the same breath he told me about experiences of frustration regarding his inability to pray and anxiety about a future retreat he was going to make.

I asked, "Do you think that what happened at midnight Mass could have been God working in you?" I invited Dean to stay with that experience and unpack it. "What do you think God was doing back there on Christmas Eve?"

Dean responded with uncharacteristic certainty, "God was showing me his love, his kindness, his gentleness, and his goodness."

"And what was God like?" I asked. "Was God far away, was he near, was he within you?"

"God was near," Dean responded, "giving me this beautiful gift."

"And what was that gift?"

Dean responded without hesitation, "That he loved me."

"God loves you," I repeated. "And what is it like to know that God loves you?"

"It's wonderful. I can't describe it."

"Dean," I asked, "what would you say to someone who came to you and told you about this experience and also told you the other things you were saying: 'I'm not good enough, I'm not holy enough, I'm anxious about the retreat I'm planning to make...'."

After a pause Dean answered, "I would tell them that all these things lead to discouragement and therefore can't be from God. *God* is saying, 'Come over here where *I* am.'"

God Is For Us

If God is for us, who is against us? He who did not with-
hold his own Son, but gave him up for all of us, will he not
with him also give us everything else? Who will bring any
charge against God's elect? It is God who justifies. Who is
to condemn? It is Christ Jesus, who died, yes, who was
raised, who is at the right hand of God, who indeed intercedes for us.

Who will separate us from the love of Christ? Will
hardship, or distress, or persecution, or famine, or nakedness, or peril, or sword? As it is written, "For your sake we
are being killed all day long; we are accounted as sheep to
be slaughtered."

No, in all these things we are more than conquerors
through him who loved us. For I am convinced that neither death, nor life, nor angels, nor rulers, nor things present, nor things to come, nor powers, nor height, nor
depth, nor anything else in all creation, will be able to separate us from the love of God in Christ Jesus our Lord.

ROMANS 8:31-39

The spiritual consolation Dean experienced at the
Eucharistic celebration on Christmas Eve led to a deeper sense
of God's presence and love for him. His other concerns, frustrations, and anxieties, "lead to discouragement and therefore
can't be from God." God was inviting Dean into relationship,
saying, as he says to all of us, "Come over here where I am."

God's Presence Now

The failure of relationship and community characterizes so
much of modern life. Without the positive experiences of inter-
personal relationship in family or community, it can be difficult
to be aware of the relationship that exists between God and us.
Today, many discover the benevolence and tenderness of
God only at the end of a dramatic, lonely journey filled with
deceptions and delusions.

Yet people desire a relationship with an objective Other, the experience of finding oneself by giving oneself away. There is a sense of dissatisfaction with radical and superficial individualism. People today want to know they belong to Someone bigger than themselves who can give their life and their love meaning.

Those moments of wonder, the sudden sense that you are not alone, the beauty that is evidence of something more—these moments of consolation are moments of relationship and prayer. They lift us out of ourselves, thrust us toward God and others, free us from the labyrinth of our own psyches and the tides of our own changeable feelings, for "we cannot truly find ourselves except through a sincere gift of ourselves to God and to others."[1]

Psalm 100

A prayer to help you give yourself joyfully to God.

> Make a joyful noise to the LORD, all the earth.
>> Worship the LORD with gladness;
>> come into his presence with singing.
>
> Know that the LORD is God.
>> It is he that made us, and we are his
>> we are his people, and the sheep of his pasture.
>
> Enter his gates with thanksgiving,
>> and his courts with praise.
>> Give thanks to him, bless his name.
>
> For the LORD is good;
>> his steadfast love endures forever,
>> and his faithfulness to all generations. (vv. 1–5)

Breaking Open Your Life

Recall spiritual consolations you have experienced—flashes of light or grace that moved you to deeper faith, a knowledge and experience of God's love, to the service of others. Start keeping a journal of these experiences and notice if there is a pattern to what God is working in your life. There is!

Notes:

[1]Second Vatican Council, *Pastoral Constitution on the Church in the Modern World, Gaudium et Spes* (Boston: Pauline Books and Media, 1999), no. 24.

CHAPTER FOURTEEN

Inner Healing Is a Spiritual Issue

Our transformation into Christ is brought about by the Holy Spirit in union with Mary, because this transformation is the continuation of the work begun on the day of the Annunciation.

—Blessed James Alberione, *The Following of Christ the Master*

Our present psychological condition owes its complexity to the drama of our personal history—from the successes and failures that have been ours, to the experiences, the lessons, the hurts and the dreams. Many good Christians are plagued with the sense that they have been ruined by the experiences of their life, by what they have done and what has been done to them. They are troubled by doubts about who they are, beneath the masks they wear. They fear they are no good, that God could never find it within himself to forgive them, much less love them.

Janice felt this way. She asked me how she could stop fearing a God who could never accept her in order to trust a God who loves her into being and surrounds her with mercy. I paused a moment, unable to respond immediately with a simple answer to her question. I had spent twenty-five years wrestling with the same issue.

However, two things stood out for us. I had discovered that I had unconsciously assumed God looked at me with the same eyes with which I looked at myself. I hated myself, therefore God hated me. I looked at myself with angry eyes, therefore God looked at me with angry eyes.

When I began to see myself differently, it seemed that God looked at me differently. One retreat, I looked in my mind's eye into the face of God and saw an angry God. I knew by then that this was untrue, that this could not be who God really is. This disparaging look could hardly be from God. So in my imagination I picked up a hammer and smashed the face. To my surprise it broke up into tiny pieces and disappeared, replaced with silence.

The Real Face of God

During supper Jesus, knowing that the Father had given all things into his hands, and that he had come from God and was going to God, got up from the table, took off his outer robe, and tied a towel around himself. Then he poured water into a basin and began to wash the disciples' feet and to wipe them with the towel that was tied around him.

He came to Simon Peter, who said to him, "Lord, are you going to wash my feet?" Jesus answered, "You do not know now what I am doing, but later you will understand." Peter said to him, "You will never wash my feet." Jesus answered, "Unless I wash you, you have no share with me." Simon Peter said to him, "Lord, not my feet only but also my hands and my head!"...

After he had washed their feet, had put on his robe, and had returned to the table, he said to them, 'Do you know what I have done to you? You call me Teacher and Lord—and you are right, for that is what I am. So if I, your Lord and Teacher, have washed your feet, you also ought to wash one another's feet.

JOHN 13:2-9, 12-14

Like Peter, we often can't see what is right in front of us. Jesus bent down and washed the apostle's feet. God did the task usually assigned to slaves. It was a lowly, humiliating, dirty job. But God wanted his apostles to see who he really is. God is the One who serves, who bends down from heaven to wash and heal. God is the One who pours out his love for his creatures. God is the One who will do more than any human would do for the love of another. God is humble. God's power is service.

Peter didn't want this kind of a God. "You will not wash my feet! I want a God who will save us from the Romans and usher in the kingdom in power and glory!" "But Peter," Jesus could have said, "this is a god of your imagination. Before you kneels the God who is. Will you accept me? Will you let me wash your feet?"

When we smash our false ideas of who God is, of how God loves, of the way God perceives us, we acquire the vision to see God as he is. We then can reread our life's complexity as salvation history. Every bit of our ups and downs is salvation, as were the ups and downs of the Israelites. Every disturbance of our personality, every failure, every mental suffering or emotional knot becomes a remembrance of God, a communication of God, and our participation in his Paschal Feast.

When we pray for inner healing, we permit Jesus to visit all those areas of our life where we have been wounded. At the base of these wounds we discover the potential for forgiveness. This is the door through which we pass in order to take up our life as filled with the love of Jesus. When we encounter the One who forgives, we forget the anguish of the past and are able to forgive ourselves.

Psalm 22

A plea to see God's true face

My God, my God, why have you forsaken me?
    Why are you so far from helping me, from the words of
        my groaning?
O my God, I cry by day, but you do not answer;
    and by night, but find no rest.
Yet you are holy,
    enthroned on the praises of Israel.
In you our ancestors trusted;
    they trusted, and you delivered them.
To you they cried, and were saved;
    in you they trusted, and were not put to shame.

But I am a worm, and not human;
    scorned by others, and despised by the people.
All who see me mock at me;
    they make mouths at me, they shake their heads;
"Commit your cause to the LORD; let him deliver—
    let him rescue the one in whom he delights!"

Yet it was you who took me from the womb;
    you kept me safe on my mother's breast.
On you I was cast from my birth,
    and since my mother bore me you have been my God.
Do not be far from me,
    for trouble is near
    and there is no one to help....

I am poured out like water,
    and all my bones are out of joint;
my heart is like wax;
    it is melted within my breast;...

I can count all my bones.
They stare and gloat over me;
they divide my clothes among themselves,
    and for my clothing they cast lots.

But you, O LORD, do not be far away!
    O my help, come quickly to my aid!...

Save me from the mouth of the lion!
From the horns of the wild oxen you have rescued me.
I will tell of your name to my brothers and sisters;
    in the midst of the congregation I will praise you:
You who fear the LORD, praise him!
    All you offspring of Jacob, glorify him;
    stand in awe of him, all you offspring of Israel!
For he did not despise or abhor
    the affliction of the afflicted;
he did not hide his face from me,
    but heard when I cried to him. (vv. 1-11, 14, 17-24)

Breaking Open Your Life

Spend some time contemplating your heart. Stay in a quiet place, play some music if you like or light a candle. Can you look confidently into the eyes of God? God wants you to look into his eyes with peace and acceptance. If it is helpful, pray before an icon, and gaze into the eyes of Jesus as depicted there.

As you look into these eyes, observe the thoughts that present themselves to you. Are they accusations? Write them down. Are they discouraging thoughts? Are they fearful thoughts? Or are they thoughts of joy, trust, and gratitude? Write them all down. Share them with a friend or spiritual director.

Tell Jesus that you want to see and believe in God's love for you. Read the parable of the Good Samaritan (Lk 10:30-37). An illuminated manuscript of the mid-sixth century, *Codex Rossanensis,* depicts Jesus as the good Samaritan tenderly nursing wounded and decaying humanity lying by the side of the road. An angel stands by Jesus, ministering to him and holding the golden bowl of grace and compassion with veiled hands. Though angels are not allowed to hold this bowl without veiling their hands, Jesus bends over and pours its contents freely upon the body and soul of his beloved brother wounded by sin.

Imagine Jesus finding you lying abandoned on the side of the road. He bends over to wash your wounds. Look into his eyes. How does Jesus look at you?

Movement Three
Abiding in Love

Transformation to a life of love means beginning to follow Jesus along a path which must take me in a direction directly opposite to self-oriented choices. It is shifting away from self-love to self-giving in love.

CHAPTER FIFTEEN

My Word Is Love

We grow in love of God as we grow in any intimate love relationship—through a continuum of knowing, trusting, desiring, surrendering our defenses and fears, and ultimately our very selves, to the Beloved.

—Thelma Hall, R.C., *Too Deep for Words: Rediscovering the Lectio Divina*

In the Gospel of John, Jesus tells his disciples, then and now, that we will touch his face and grasp his hand when we abide in him and believe his word. The word becomes our way to love and to life. We can taste no joy more complete than this abiding in love, this fulfillment of the promise: "My Father will love them, and we will come to them and make our home with them" (Jn 14:23).

Also in the Gospel of John, Jesus invites his apostles and disciples (including us) to abide in his word. "If you abide in my Word…you are truly my disciples, and you will know the truth, and the truth will set you free" (Jn 8:31-32 AMP). Abiding in the Word, therefore, allows us to know truth. With the truth, we can enter into right relationships with God and with others. Without the truth we live in an endlessly distorted illusion, perhaps fooling others, certainly fooling ourselves.

What is this truth about which Jesus speaks? The antiphon for the Magnificat of Vespers on December 28th defines it: "The holy Virgin gave birth to God who became for us the frail, tender baby she nursed at her breast. Let us worship the God who came to save us." God revealed in Jesus, born to live in solidarity with all humanity and each human person, this is the God in whom we abide through faith and worship. This mutual abiding is the dance of salvation.

Actively Abiding

Reading Scripture, therefore, is more than a search for information or even inspiration. Reading becomes an abiding in the eternal Word of God. Abiding is more than an intellectual or sentimental communion. To abide is to open ourselves to God's transforming action present in the Word.

Whether we are consciously aware of it or not, we desire change, conversion, transformation of life. We read the pages of Scripture with the desire to more completely embody the likeness of Christ, to radiate his thoughts, his desires, his words, his actions, his preferences, his motivations. In the words of the church fathers, we want to become "a son in the Son." We desire nothing less than to be dismantled so that we might be created anew.

To approach the Word, to present our souls for this act of creation, our hearts must be readied, the ground must be prepared. God creates always *ex nihilo*, out of nothing (Gn 1). God can create us anew out of our sinfulness, illnesses of spirit, addictive behaviors, or stubborn attitudes.

We do not have to be holy to approach the Word that divinizes us. We do need, however, to read with a contemplative gaze. The philosopher Simone Weil, understanding the power of the contemplative heart, wrote: *"Le regard est ce qui sauve"*—"gazing is what saves." We must read Scripture with the attitude of Mary who remained at the Lord's feet, under his loving gaze, never removing herself from his influence over her. Abiding in the Word is remaining in this radius of watchfulness.

Abiding in the Word implies an activity sustained over a period of time. It calls for repetition and perseverance. Scripture often lulls us into a sweet satisfaction, drawing us back again and again to the sweetness of its revelation. It holds out the intriguing promise of Jesus, "But those who drink of the water that I will give them will never be thirsty again" (Jn 4:14). The only adequate answer to this biblical summons is the response of the Samaritan woman, "Sir, give me this water so that I may never be thirsty" (Jn 4:15). We will not understand Scripture until we thirst for it with the agonizing thirst of one who has journeyed through the desert and found no other satisfactory source of water.

The Work of the Spirit

Abiding in the Word is only possible if Scripture is read under the power of the Spirit. In sacred Scripture, God speaks to us in a human way. To interpret Scripture correctly, we must "be attentive to what the human authors truly wanted to affirm, and to what God wanted to reveal to us by their words."[1] Reading commentaries can help us avoid twisting Scripture to mean what we think it means.

> In order to discover the sacred authors' intention, the reader must take into account the conditions of their time and culture, the literary genres in use at that time, and the modes of feeling, speaking and narrating then current. "For the fact is that truth is differently presented and expressed in the various types of historical writing, in prophetical and poetical texts, and in other forms of literary expression."[2]

However, it isn't necessary to wade through exegetical essays to grasp this material. A short reading from a good commentary is sufficient. All of this serves to sharpen our ears so that

we might hear the truth free from distortions created by ignorance. But it is through the Spirit's power, quickening our souls,
that we are re-created.

Consider the story of Philip and the eunuch (Acts, chapter 8). The Spirit told Philip to catch up with the carriage of a
court official from Ethiopia. As he caught up with the
Ethiopian, Philip heard him reading from the prophet Isaiah.
Philip called out to him, "Do you understand what you are reading?" (Acts 8:30). The Ethiopian official responded that it was
impossible to understand what he was reading because he had
no one to explain it to him. "Then Philip began to speak, and
starting with this scripture, he proclaimed to him the good
news about Jesus" (Acts 8:35).

The Holy Spirit transforms printed words into proclamation. Such proclamation leads to commitment, and a transfer of
loyalties. "Look," pointed out the eunuch, "here is water. What
is to prevent me from being baptized?…[B]oth of them, Philip
and the eunuch, went down into the water, and Philip baptized
him"(Acts 8:36-38).

Through baptism and the sacramental life we become, as
it were, the property of a new Master. Paul states of the baptized, "You are not your own…you were bought with a price"
(1 Cor 6:19-20). "Those who belong to Christ" (1 Cor 15:23, Gal
5:24) cannot return to their former master. The One who has
paid the price of emancipation requires that we be faithful to his
worship and his service.

The justification Christ brings is given as "a gift, through
the redemption that is in Christ Jesus, whom God put forward
as a sacrifice of atonement by his blood, effective through faith"
(Rom 3:24-25). There has been, in effect, a transfer of ownership. Those who once were slaves have a new standing and now
belong to Jesus Christ.

Abiding in the Word implies a deepening relationship. We
do more than think through the meaning of the message, we

respond to some facet of God's love which is revealed to us. Thinking is a process in which we move from one idea to another. Listening is a receptive act during which we absorb the fact that we are loved. Borrowing Jesuit Father Peter Hannon's phrase, when we think, we obtain good advice from Scripture. When we listen, we receive the good news that someone loves us and affirms us.

Finally, when we abide in the Word we discover that it has the power to overturn human prejudice and pride, to turn our self-centeredness inside out, to transform our ignorance and foolishness into divine Wisdom. The often-paradoxical statements create in our heart earth-shattering reverberations and our all-too-natural logic crumbles. The only way to understand the Word is to live it. Reading by itself will never allow us to grasp the divine logic of God becoming one of us to save us. The risk of living what we read reveals to us the truth that sets us free.

Note:

[1]*Catechism of the Catholic Church*, 2nd ed.(Washington, D.C.: USCCB, 1997), no. 109.
[2]*Ibid.*, no. 110.

CHAPTER SIXTEEN

Primer on Methods of Prayer

Our own spirit already tells us that we are limited and that God alone can help us...by...meeting us on the way.
—Adrienne Von Speyr, *The Victory of Love: A Meditation on Romans 8*

Here we are, then, desiring to pray, yet finding ourselves trapped in our imagination, distractions, fatigue, boredom, fears, and emotional knots. How do we calm ourselves, smooth out the wrinkles of our cares and worries, and focus on Someone other than ourselves? There are exercises we can do to help us prepare for prayer.

My brother-in-law, who has four young boys and a full-time job, has gone back to school for an MBA. When he studies, he goes into a room apart from where the kids are playing. He may reread his past notes as he gets himself into the frame of mind to concentrate on his assignments. Gradually he slows down, and the voices of the children get farther and farther away. Additionally, before his classes, he goes for a swim to help him leave behind his workday and switch from functional to receptive thinking. Because we are human, we need rituals that get us in the right frame of mind for what we plan to do next.

Similarly, there are also good habits we can acquire that will make us more receptive to prayer. Preparatory exercises are good habits that make contemplative, transforming prayer possible. Try the various exercises that follow and settle on those that leave you feeling most serene. These exercises work best when they become habits, that is, when they are used consistently and gently.

Preparation

Peace

Sit down comfortably while keeping a straight back. Place your hands on your knees, open, with the palms up.

Take three long breaths, letting the air out with a slight sigh. For about one minute, repeat slowly to yourself words such as: Peace. Be calm. Let everything go. Relax.

Gently notice your shoulders, neck, arms, hands, stomach. Invite them to relax. Feel them relax. Observe the movement of your lungs, the beating of your heart. Tell these two great organs of your body to relax now.

Picture in your mind a straight line. The present moment is positioned right in the middle. The present moment is now, and now, and now, with each breath. Begin to erase what's on the line to the left of the present moment: erase memories, fear, noises, other voices. To the right of the line is the future: erase ideas, plans, fears, expectations. Erase everything so that only the present moment remains, a moment that lets go of the past with each breath, and welcomes the future for just the space of a breath, until you let that go also.

Remain in the present. Breathe gently and remain in the present moment for about thirty seconds. Relax for a moment, and then return to the image of the line and the present breath again for thirty seconds. Relax again, and then return to the image of the present moment and your breath.

Interior Emptiness

Close your eyes and imagine the face of a clock. Very slowly follow the second hand as it moves around the clock. Open your eyes and rest. Once again close your eyes and imagine the face of a clock. Again follow the second hand around the face of the clock, but this time let the second hand stop at each second, gradually slowing down and remaining motionless at each second before moving on. Open your eyes. Once again, in your imagination, observe the second hand moving even more slowly around the face of the clock. At the end you should feel quiet and empty.

Serenity

After doing the prayer preparation for peace, above, begin to stop all mental activity. Imagine all your thoughts and ideas emptying out of the base of your neck like sand in an hourglass. Rest a moment, then once again feel your mind and imagination emptying out. Experience your whole being as if there were no thoughts, images, emotions, preoccupations; nothing grabbling for your attention.

Gazing

Very calmly enter into your soul. What is it like there? Calm? Bright? Peaceful? Comforting? Safe? Continue gazing gently until you have left behind the distractions around you, until you are aware of only your presence and the presence of God. These two presences are moving toward each other, seeking each other out, desiring each other, loving each other. Remain in the presence of God.

A Method of Lectio Divina

When we immerse ourselves in Scripture through frequent prayerful reading of the words of God, we become open to the divine Teacher who gives us the "kiss of eternity" (William of St. Thierry), slakes our spiritual thirst, and enables us to experience the saving power of God. An ancient Benedictine method of reading and meditating on the Word of God, *lectio divina*, bears fruit through faithfulness sustained over months and years.

Preparation

Choose a passage of Scripture for your day's prayer. It could be the passage from the readings in the daily Eucharist, or a passage in a consecutive reading of one of the books of the Bible. Prepare a quiet place where you can pray for about twenty minutes if that is possible for your schedule. If not, give this practice as much time as you can, even if you have to break it up between ten minutes in the morning and ten minutes in the evening. As you begin your prayer, take a few seconds to quiet and center your mind, relax your body, and open your heart.

Lectio (Read)

To begin the Lectio, read the passage you have chosen. It is helpful to read it several times, making a quiet act of reverence between each reading such as kissing the pages of Scripture, bowing, making a sign of the cross, turning your hands palms up in a gesture of supplication. Between each reading do not try to figure out what it means, simply remain in silence. Read it quietly aloud at least one time. Repeat several times a word or a phrase that impresses you.

Meditatio (Ponder)

By now you should be much quieter, and the phrase that struck you should be more deeply rooted in your heart as you repeat it. Take note of words and images that begin to surface. Turn the words around curiously in your mind. Reflect on why they stood out for you today and how they might offer you direction in the affairs of your day. Ponder the passage until a prayer begins to spontaneously form in your heart.

Orare (Pray)

As your heart spontaneously begins to speak to God about what you have pondered, open yourself to the Lord. Speak directly to God. Sometimes the prayer will be one of repentance, other times it will be one of praise, joy, thanksgiving, petition, adoration, love. Follow the direction of your heart.

Contemplatio (Contemplation)

Allow your heart to fall into silence, into a kind of sustained gazing between you and God. God holds you with his gaze, and you slowly grow strong enough to gaze into these eyes that so unabashedly express to you their love and welcome. Remain as long as possible in this quiet space without words or images when they are not needed, returning to them when they seem necessary.

Actio (Action)

As you finish your prayer, tuck into your memory the phrase that caused the deepest reaction in you, and which now will be your companion throughout the day. Pray it over and over on the bus, before meetings, when worried about your son who isn't home from school on time. Scripture become a thread intertwined throughout your day, giving it new meaning and hope.

A Method of Centering Prayer

Centering prayer is a wordless opening of the mind and heart to God which facilitates the development of contemplative prayer. Centering prayer presupposes the action of God within us, and through the frequent practice of this prayer we discover the powerful presence of God which we often take for granted. It is as if we say "yes" to everything God is and does within us.

Choose a Sacred Word

Ask the Holy Spirit to inspire you with a word that you can use when you pray. This sacred word is a symbol of your intention to remain open to God's presence and action. Examples are: Jesus, love, Abba, peace, nothing.

Begin to Pray

Make sure you are relaxed and in a quiet place. You can set an alarm for twenty minutes, which is a suggested period for this type of prayer. Close your eyes and begin to pray your word gently, as if you were placing a light feather on your hand.

Thoughts

When you become aware of thoughts, feelings, or memories, return to your prayer word. The word becomes the simple means by which you return to "the center" in your prayer, since it is the business of the mind to range about, curious and interested in everything. Thoughts are a normal part of prayer. Don't try to get rid of them, swatting them like flies. With the slightest expenditure of energy, simply restate your prayer word. Every time your mind wanders, pull it back with your prayer word. By returning to your word, you return to your centered presence in God.

After the Prayer Time

Slowly recite the Our Father, look about you while you remain in silence, or quietly begin to reintroduce the tasks of the day into your consciousness. As much as possible, try to take the quiet of this prayer with you during the day.

A Method of Ignatian Prayer

Ignatian contemplation is an affective method of prayer that engages all the human faculties. This form of contemplation is often called imaginative prayer because we begin by placing ourselves imaginatively in the scene of a Gospel passage as we try to engage God's mystery. Through encountering God personally within the context of the Gospel, we grow in faith as we experience God's presence and mystery.

After reading the Bible passage selected for meditation, St. Ignatius invites us to imagine ourselves as one of the characters in the story. Using all our senses, we can allow ourselves to see, hear, smell, and touch each facet of the event. As we experience the gospel scene, we become aware of how we respond on a feeling level and we consider what it means for us at this time.

Preparation

Find a time and a place conducive to prayer. If you would like, light a candle, burn some incense, or place a favorite icon on the table. Choose a passage of the Gospel for meditation. When you are first learning how to pray in this way, stories from the Gospel will be the easiest to use because they include details, words, and actions of Jesus or those who were interacting with him.

It is typical of Ignatian prayer that you first ask God for what you desire in your prayer. It may be to love God more deeply, to understand the love of Jesus for you, to find an answer to a particular problem. Whatever it is, state it directly to God.

Read the Passage

Read the passage, imagining the setting as vividly as you can. Read the passage several times. Now place the Bible aside.

What are the sounds in the story? Is someone talking? Are they raising their voice or whispering? How is this voice coming across to you? What is happening in the Gospel scene? What do you see? What are the people doing? How are they dressed? What role might you choose in this story? What else is happening in the scene?

Place yourself in the scene. Are you one of the characters in the story? What are you doing there? What are your feelings?

Imagine the people, the place, the dust, the smell, the objects, the animals, the words spoken, and so on. Just let yourself go. Enjoy the scene. You are not a bystander or an onlooker. Be active in what is happening! It is almost like daydreaming.

Talk to the characters in the story. Talk to Jesus about what he is doing. Is there anything you want to ask him?

Does he ask you anything? Listen to what Jesus says to you. What are you feeling? Sometimes in your prayer the story can change and take unexpected twists. Allow this to happen. Often something very significant is revealed to us in the changes.

Spend Time in the Company of Jesus

Do not moralize or try to make applications, just be present to the scene. Do not try to reason out or learn. Be content just be there. Spend time in the company of Jesus. Talk to him and thank him for all that happened or did not happen during the prayer.

Close with the Our Father and offer yourself to God.

Keep a Journal of Your Experience

Write about your experience in a journal, paying close attention to your feelings. What struck you most in your prayer?

St. Ignatius recommends that after a period of prayer, the person spend some time reviewing and reflecting on how the prayer went. Was it alive? Dry? Was I too tired? Distracted? Moved? Become familiar with the way in which God deals with you. In subsequent times of prayer return to the same passage of Scripture as long as it is life-giving. When there seems to be no more to gain from that passage, then move on. It is very fruitful to share your prayer and the journal of your feelings with a spiritual director.

A Method of Eucharistic Prayer

Eucharistic adoration is an increasingly popular form of prayer among young people and within parishes. The time spent in adoration, keeping Jesus company, or simply in silent personal prayer and reading is immensely fruitful and satisfying. Although there is no one right way to spend time in Eucharistic adoration, the Pauline form of the "Visit" with Jesus, or the Hour of Adoration, is a life-giving model. (Pauline refers to the men's and women's religious congregations founded by Blessed James Alberione.)

Rather than a succession of prayers, the "Visit" to Jesus is meant to be just that, a visit, a time when you share everything about your life with Jesus and place yourself before him so that he can teach you, heal you, guide you, and love you. Although it is presented in three steps, often these phases of the visit blend into one long conversation.

1.) Adoration of Jesus Master, the One Who Reveals to Us the Inner Reality of God

Jesus is the Truth, who reveals God to us and us to ourselves. Begin the visit by quieting your mind and heart. Tell Jesus what is going on in your life, your fears, your joys, your worries, your desires. Tell him everything.

Jesus reveals himself to us today through Scripture and in the story of our life. Take some time to read the Bible. Select a book of the Bible to read through consecutively or follow the readings chosen for the Eucharistic liturgy. In your reading, Jesus is responding to all you have shared with him of your life. He is speaking to you directly, not to the people who lived two thousand years ago. He wants to tell you something very particular, a message he has for no one else.

2.) Adoration of Jesus Master, the One Who Confronts Our Life and Makes It Possible for Us to Receive a New Origin through Rebirth

Jesus is the way and the goal. By believing the revelation of Jesus, we are on the way. When we surrender our criteria for what is truth, our ideas of the way to find God and happiness, our self-made idols, we arrive at a true self-understanding. As creatures who are loved and saved, we can put our faith entirely in the word Jesus speaks to us. Allow what you have read, what Jesus has revealed to you already in your time of prayer,to arouse your heart to repentance, to create great desires, to strengthen your resolve.

How can you center more on Jesus' way? Where do you follow your own way? Jesus will continually stand before you as the One who asks if you believe in him, in his revelation of the Father, in his dream for you.

3.) Adoration of Jesus Master, the One Who Gives Us Light and Life

Jesus alone gives us access to God who is the life that we so desperately seek. Jesus is the way; he is the divine reality that bestows the life through which humanity finds its proper relation to the Creator. Jesus bestows grace and truth that we might share in the fullness of God's divine being.

Spend the remainder of your time of adoration in the prayer that most expresses your love for Jesus and trust in his power in your life. You could pray the psalms or the Liturgy of the Hours. You might recite the rosary or read favorite prayers. You may also want to spend the rest of the time in complete trusting silence, allowing Jesus to speak to your heart on a level deeper than words and images. Jesus will lead you to life-giving prayer and to Life itself.

CHAPTER SEVENTEEN

Opening Your Future to Love

In everything that befalls Jacob, he experiences not himself but the way of God.

> —Adrienne Von Speyr, *The Mission of the Prophets*

T he following Scripture verses and meditations are designed to stimulate prayer and provide a pattern for coming before the Lord through the words of the Bible.

Psalm 46

A psalm to pray when feeling vulnerable.

> God is our refuge and strength,
>   a very present help in trouble.
> Therefore we will not fear, though the earth should
>   change,
>   though the mountains shake in the heart of the sea;
> though its waters roar and foam,
>   though the mountains tremble with its
>   tumult.   *Selah*
>
> There is a river whose streams make glad the city of God,
>   the holy habitation of the Most High.
> God is in the midst of the city; it shall not be moved;
>   God will help it when the morning dawns.

The nations are in an uproar, the kingdoms totter;
>   he utters his voice, the earth melts.
The LORD of hosts is with us;
>   the God of Jacob is our refuge. (vv. 1-7)   *Selah*

This psalm is about vulnerability. Israel believed there were two things that could destroy them: the sea and their surrounding neighbors. The water was always trying to topple the mountains which ancients believed went deep into the ocean and held up the land. People were anxious about the primeval chaos of the waters, the threat that the waters might break in upon the land and destroy them. Israel was also vulnerable because stronger nations attacked and pillaged them.

It is when we feel anxiety over potential calamity that we should call out to God in faith. Psalm 46 expresses our faith, our utter dependence on God, in spite of circumstances, even circumstances as devastating as the death of a loved one or financial disaster. No matter what catastrophe affects our lives, "The Lord of hosts is with us; the God of Jacob is our stronghold."

A comforting passage for times when you feel unworthy.

One of the Pharisees asked Jesus to eat with him, and he went into the Pharisee's house and took his place at the table. And a woman in the city, who was a sinner, having learned that he was eating in the Pharisee's house, brought an alabaster jar of ointment. She stood behind him at his feet, weeping, and began to bathe his feet with her tears and to dry them with her hair. Then she continued kissing his feet and anointing them with the ointment....

[Jesus] said to her, "Your sins are forgiven." But those who were at the table with him began to say among themselves, "Who is this who even forgives sins?" And he said to the woman, "Your faith has saved you; go in peace."

LUKE 7:36-38, 48-50

Jesus' arrival in town deeply affected this woman. He was dining at Simon's house, a religious leader who perceived himself as good, especially when compared to this woman who in her sin presented herself to Jesus. The presence of the all-holy One attracts those who know themselves to be impure, broken, blemished, fallen. This woman is drawn to him, she doesn't run and hide in his presence like Adam and Eve in the garden. She comes openly with her sin into the presence of Jesus. Because she trusts, because she makes herself available to grace, she finds that God will deal with his children who are both good and bad, graced and fallen, who take time to grow, who need many opportunities and much mercy before they can stand in the brightness of his love.

Judging others prevents us from embracing the truth about creation.

> Do not judge, so that you may not be judged. For with the judgment you make you will be judged, and the measure you give will be the measure you get.
>
> MATTHEW 7:1-2

There is an important nuance in the Greek rendering of this passage: though we may stop judging others, they will not stop judging us. Judging others is a way of assuring our own survival. If we can assure ourselves that others are not as good, as fast, as talented, as successful as ourselves, then we can rest in the illusion we have created.

Ceasing to judge implies that we allow ourselves to be dethroned, to be vulnerable, to be unimportant, brushed aside, and marginalized. When we refuse to judge, we restore the Lord to the center of our sphere of influence. We can be assured that the Lord will not be like the others. He alone is our final judge but right here, right now, he calls to us, stands by us, and draws us to himself in love and forgiveness.

The alternative to being judged is being forgiven,

understood, embraced. By not judging, we restore the original blueprint for creation and we find ourselves walking familiarly with a God we can trust.

A reflection for a time when you feel unexpecedly forgiven.

> After this he went out and saw a tax collector named Levi, sitting at the tax booth; and he said to him, "Follow me." And he got up, left everything, and followed him.
>
> Then Levi gave a great banquet for him in his house; and there was a large crowd of tax collectors and others sitting at the table with them. The Pharisees and their scribes were complaining to his disciples, saying, "Why do you eat and drink with tax collectors and sinners?" Jesus answered, "Those who are well have no need of a physician, but those who are sick; I have come to call not the righteous but sinners to repentance."
>
> LUKE 5:27-33

Tax collectors were regarded as traitors and enemies of the God of Israel. When Jesus called Levi to be his disciple, people must have been shocked. Why did Jesus do this? Did he see something more in Levi than a money monger? Levi could not believe that such a righteous and holy person as Jesus would call him. His response was instantaneous. Levi didn't use his new influence to snub his friends. He realized that if Jesus could welcome him, he had no right to turn his back on his outcast companions.

So he invited Jesus to a meal with his friends and introduced Jesus to them. Table fellowship is a sign of full acceptance. Jesus' presence at that meal emphasized that he considered them worthy of his companionship.

A prayer for Christian conviction.

> Simon Peter answered him, "Lord to whom can we go? You have the words of eternal life. We have come to believe and know that you are the Holy One of God."
>
> JOHN 6:68-69

This passage concludes John's account of the separation that occurred among the group of disciples following the "hard sayings" of Jesus. The revelation is a call to a decision, to an act of faith affirming that God meets us in the claim of Jesus of Nazareth.

Peter's response is an act of decision. It is not a lucky guess or a profound insight. It is the answer of one who responds to the revelation with *belief,* an answer which is in some way dependent upon the revelation. Peter's declaration, *"You are the Holy One of God,"* is a clear formulation of faith. Peter affirms that Jesus belongs to God and stands over against the world. Jesus' special relation to God is expressed in the fact that he is *the* holy One of God, the one and only holy One.

At the same time, Peter's title for Jesus expresses that Jesus is also *for* the world: Jesus represents God in the world as the One who reveals God to the world, for the sake of the world, and who thus offers the life to the world.

A passage for those struggling with faith.

> When he entered Capernaum, a centurion came to him, appealing to him and saying, "Lord, my servant is lying at home paralyzed, in terrible distress." And he said to him, "I will come and cure him." The centurion answered, "Lord, I am not worthy to have you come under my roof; but only speak the word, and my servant will be healed. For I also am a man under authority, with soldiers under me; and I say to one, 'Go,' and he goes, and to another, 'Come,' and he comes, and to my slave, 'Do this,' and the slave does it."
>
> When Jesus heard him, he was amazed and said to those who followed him, "Truly I tell you, in no one in Israel have I found such faith. I tell you, many will come from east and west and will eat with Abraham and Isaac and Jacob in the kingdom of heaven, while the heirs of the kingdom will be thrown into the outer darkness, where there will be weeping and gnashing of teeth."

> And to the centurion Jesus said, "Go; let it be done for you according to your faith." And the servant was healed in that hour.
>
> MATTHEW 8:5-13

In the Gospel of Matthew, the faith that Jesus approves is often exhibited, not by his disciples, but by those outside the circle of his followers. In contrast, the disciples are sometimes rebuked for their lack of faith as when Jesus tells his disciples, "But if God so clothes the grass of the field, which is alive today and tomorrow is thrown into the oven, will he not much more clothe you—you of little faith?" (Mt. 6:30). Even after the Resurrection his disciples still doubt.

In Matthew, therefore, faith is not seen as a prerequisite for discipleship but as the goal. Struggles with doubt are part and parcel of our life when we strive to grow in faith.

A word of courage for those times you feel you aren't good enough.

> Therefore, to keep me from being too elated, a thorn was given me in the flesh, a messenger of Satan to torment me, to keep me from being too elated. Three times I appealed to the Lord about this, that it would leave me, but he said to me, "My grace is sufficient for you, for power is made perfect in weakness." So, I will boast all the more gladly of my weaknesses, so that the power of Christ may dwell in me. Therefore I am content with weaknesses, insults, hardships, persecutions, and calamities for the sake of Christ; for whenever I am weak, then I am strong.
>
> 2 CORINTHIANS 12:7-10

A *theology of weakness* characterizes Paul's apostolic spirituality. A search for the word "weakness" in the Revised Standard Version of the Bible brings up ten uses of the word. All ten are in the New Testament and seven of these are in Paul (the remaining three are in Hebrews).

He speaks of *weakness in prayer*: "Likewise the Spirit

helps us in our weakness; for we do not know how to pray as we ought, but that very Spirit intercedes with sighs too deep for words" (Rom 8:26). Of *God's weakness*: "For God's foolishness is wiser than human wisdom, and God's weakness is stronger than human strength" (1 Cor 1:25).

Weakness as a characteristic of his apostolic style: "And I came to you in weakness and in fear and in much trembling" (1 Cor 2:3).

The weakness of the present body as opposed to the body of the resurrection: "It is sown in dishonor, it is raised in glory. It is sown in weakness, it is raised in power" (1 Cor 15:43).

His acceptance of *his own weakness* as a source of apostolic power: "If I must boast, I will boast of the things that show my weakness" (2 Cor 11:30), and "but [the Lord] said to me, 'My grace is sufficient for you, for power is made perfect in weakness.' So, I will boast all the more gladly of my weaknesses, so that the power of Christ may dwell in me" (2 Cor 12:9).

And finally of *Jesus' weakness*: "For he was crucified in weakness, but lives by the power of God. For we are weak in him, but in dealing with you we will live with him by the power of God" (2 Cor 13:4).

Instead of searching for power, prestige, and position, Christians should be relishing our weakness, poverty, and dependence. For truly it is God who will do any good in us, if we stay out of the way and turn ourselves completely over to him in trust.

A celebration of baptism and grace.

> There is therefore now no condemnation for those who are in Christ Jesus. For the law of the Spirit of life in Christ Jesus has set you free from the law of sin and of death.
>
> ROMANS 8:1-2

For Paul the death and resurrection of Christ was a cosmic event that signaled the end of the old age and the beginning of the new. The whole created order has been made new. Through the cross, God put an end to the *kosmos* of sin and death and brought into being a new *kosmos*. The old age is passing away (cf. 1 Cor 7:31b), the new age has appeared in Christ.

The foremost language Paul uses to express this cosmic reality is the abundant "in Christ" language that is found in his letters. Paul uses the phrase "in Christ" 164 times in his letters, ample evidence that he included the whole Christian life in this little phrase.

Paul's use of "in Christ" terminology embraces all of Christian existence. To be "in Christ" means to exist within a new historical order brought about by Christ's victory over the powers of sin and death. The justification brought by Christ is given as "a gift, through the redemption that is in Christ Jesus, whom God put forward as a sacrifice of atonement by his blood, effective through faith" (Rom 3.24-25). There has been, in effect, a transfer of ownership. Those who once were slaves have a new standing and become the property of Jesus Christ.

Bibliography

Commentaries on Scripture

Scripture will continue to yield its treasures as you read it prayerfully, listen to it proclaimed in the liturgy, and study it. The following commentaries on the Bible might help you in your studies:

Barclay, William, ed. The Daily Study Bible Series, rev. ed. Louisville, Ky.: Westminster John Knox Press.

Collegeville Bible Commentary Series. Collegeville, Minn.: Liturgical Press.

Leiva-Merikakis, Erasmo. *Fire of Mercy, Heart of the Word: Meditations on the Gospel According to Saint Matthew.* San Francisco: Ignatius Press, 1996.

Meditation and Commentaries (for each of the Gospels). Huntington, Ind.: Our Sunday Visitor.

Sacra Pagina Series. Collegeville, Minn.: Glazier/Liturgical Press.

Six Weeks with the Bible Series. Chicago: Loyola Press.

Books on Prayer

Arico, Carl. *A Taste of Silence: A Guide to the Fundamentals of Centering Prayer.* New York: Continuum, 2003.

Downey, Michael. *Altogether Gift: A Trinitarian Spirituality.* Maryknoll, N.Y.: Orbis, 2000.

Dubay, Thomas. *Prayer Primer: Igniting a Fire Within.* Ann Arbor, Mich.: Servant Publications, 2002.

Funk, Mary Margaret. *Tools Matter for Practicing the Spiritual Life.* New York: Continuum, 2001.

Gire, Ken. *The Work of His Hands.* Ann Arbor, Mich.: Servant, 2002.

Guardini, Romano. *The Art of Praying: The Principles and Methods of Christian Prayer.* Manchester, N.H.: Sophia Institute Press, 1994.

Harmer, Catherine M. *New Paths to God: Moving Forward on the Spiritual Journey.* Mystic, Conn.: Twenty-Third Publications, 2002.

Hynes, Mary. *Surrender: Your Way to Spiritual Health and Freedom.* Cincinnati: St. Anthony Messenger Press, 1999.

Kirvan, John. *God Hunger: Discovering the Mystic in All of Us.* Notre Dame, Ind.: Sorin Books, 1999.

Leiva-Merikakis, Erasmo. *The Way of the Disciple.* Ft. Collins, Colo.: Ignatius Press, 2003.

Miller, Robert J. *Surprised by Love: Lectio Divina Series.* Lanham, Md.: Rowman & Littlefield, Sheed and Ward, 2002.

Reilly, O.S.B., Archabbot Lambert. *Latin Sayings for Spiritual Growth.* Huntington, Ind.: Our Sunday Visitor, 2001.

Shannon, William H. *Silence on Fire: The Prayer of Awareness.* New York: Crossroad, 2000.

Smith, Natalie. *Stand on Your Own Feet: Finding a Contemplative Spirit in Everyday Life.* Notre Dame, Ind.: Thomas More Publishing, 2002.

Stinissen, Wilfried. *Praying the Name of Jesus: The Ancient Wisdom of the Jesus Prayer.* Liguori, Mo.: Ligouri, 1999.

St. Romain, Philip. *Caring for the Self, Caring for the Soul: A Book of Spiritual Development*. Liguori, Mo.: Ligouri, 2000.

Underhill, Evelyn. *Mystics of the Church*. Harrisburg, Pa.: Morehouse Publishing, 1988

————. *The Ways of the Spirit*. New York: Crossroad, 1993.

Vandergrift, Nicki Verploegen. *Organic Spirituality: A Sixfold Path for Contemplative Living*. Maryknoll, N.Y.: Orbis, 2000.

Williams, Rowan. *Ponder These Things: Praying with Icons of the Virgin*. Lanham, Md.: Rowman & Littlefield, Sheed and Ward, 2002.

Other Sources

Alberione, Blessed James. *The Following of Christ the Master*. Daughters of St. Paul, unpublished translation.

Barks, Coleman, trans. *The Essential Rumi*. San Francisco: HarperSanFrancisco, 1994.

Bonhoeffer, Dietrich. *True Patriotism: Letters, Lectures, and Notes, 1939-1945*. New York: Harper & Row, 1973.

Brother Lawrence of the Resurrection. *The Practice of the Presence of God*. New York: Image Doubleday, 1977.

Burrows, Ruth. *Ascent to Love: The Spiritual Teaching of St. John of the Cross*. Denville, N.J.: Dimension Books, 1987.

Chittister, Joan, O.S.B. *Seeing With Our Souls: Monastic Wisdom for Every Day*. Lanham, Md.: Rowman & Littlefield, Sheed and Ward, 2002.

De Caussade, Jean-Pierre. *Abandonment to Divine Providence*. New York: Doubleday Image, 1974.

Emerson, Ralph Waldo. *Essays: First and Second Series*. New York: Vintage Press, 1990.

Hall, Thelma, R.C. *Too Deep for Words: Rediscovering Lectio Divina*. New York: Paulist Press, 1988.

Hillesum, Etty. *The Interrrupted Life: The Diaries of Etty Hillesum 1941–43.* New York: Pocket Books, Washington Square Press, 1981.

Hustad, Donald P., ed. *The Worshiping Church: A Hymnal.* Carol Stream, Ill.: Hope Publishing Co., 1991.

Keating, Thomas. *Active Meditations for Contemplative Prayer.* New York: Continuum, 1997.

———. *Invitation to Love: The Way of Christian Contemplation.* New York: Continuum, 1994.

Ladinsky, Daniel, trans. *The Gift: Poems by Hafiz, the Great Sufi Master.* New York: Penguin, 1999.

Stein, Edith. *The Science of the Cross (Collected Works of Edith Stein, Vol. 6).* Washington, D.C.: ICS Publications, 2003.

Von Speyr, Adrienne. *The Mission of the Prophets.* San Francisco: Ignatius Press, 1996.

———. *The Victory of Love: A Meditation on Romans 8.* San Francisco: Ignatius Press, 1990.